CLIPPINGS FROM THE 'EDGES

This book is dedicated to the memory of
Irene Pryor 1915-2005

Cover design by Brian Maudsley

First published in 2006
by Lowedges Writers' Workshop

© Lowedges Writers' Workshop, 2006

ISBN 1 84387 179 3

Typeset by Women's Print (0114) 2669828

Printed in the UK by B & B Press (Parkgate), Rotherham.

All rights reserved. No part of this publication may be reproduced, stored in a retrieval system, or transmitted, in any form or by any means, electronic, mechanical, photocopying, recording or otherwise, without the prior permission of the publisher.

In October, 2003, I got a call from Lowedges. I was asked if I could take over a Creative Writing class. They were two weeks into a ten-week course. It was on Monday mornings. I checked my diary and said, sure, I could do it. When I asked what had happened to the teacher who'd started the course, I was told: They ran him off!

   I can still remember driving to Lowedges on that first Monday, stomach churning, thinking "What am I letting myself in for here?" Well, I found out soon enough: sheer delight. Nearly three years later, I'm still delighted, and proud to be presenting here the fruits of their labours.

Linda Lee Welch
April, 2006

Acknowledgements

We wish to thank our tutor, Linda Lee Welch, for her patience, encouragement and pushiness (in the nicest sense). Without her there wouldn't be a book. Also Roisin Birks from Lowedges Community and Safety Forum for her support and invaluable help in securing funding; Brian Mawdsley for his delightful art work and cover design; Liz Kettle from South Yorkshire Community Foundation for her guidance in the early stages of applying for funds; Gill Dyal and Krista Joel of Lowedges CSF for typing and photocopying.

This publication was made possible by grants from South Yorkshire Community Foundation and the Neighbourhood Renewal Community Chest, for which we are very grateful.

Many thanks to Sheffield Hallam University for the ISBN and practical support.

And finally, a special word for Pat Bestall, whose energy and commitment are a major driving force in the Lowedges community.

Contents

Lowedges	Bet Bullock	7
Lowedges is a Pineapple	Roisin Birks	7
Fuchsia Land	Jean Allen	9
Prayer	Jean Allen	11
Morning in Lowedges	Jean Allen	12
Early Lowedges Recollections	Win Francis	13
Gateshead	Barbara Thackeray	16
The Key	Minnie Douglas	20
Gone But Not Forgotten	Sue Roberts	21
Drugs	Irene Ward	24
Home	Pat Bestall	25
Wreck-Tangle	Dave Lightfoot	26
The Terminus Cafe	Jean Allen	29
Daffodil	Win Francis	36
Faith	Barbara Thackeray	37
Stuff Happens	Bet Bullock	38
The Mercenary	Jean Allen	44
Rain	Bet Bullock	53
Love Poem	Bet Bullock	54
Valentine	Bet Bullock	54
Sweet Mystery Of Life	Bet Bullock	55
Just Another Day	Win Francis	56
The Stand-in	Barbara Thackeray	60
The Grand Prix	Jean Allen	61
The Odd Couple	Win Francis	62
Archway	Minnie Douglas	62
Grandfather	Barbara Thackeray	63
The Wishing Well	Sue Roberts	66
Hysterectomy	Sue Roberts	67
Lanzarote	Jean Allen	68
Myths: Ancient And Modern	Bet Bullock	73
Silver Birch	Win Francis	83

Prayer	Win Francis	84
Good Samaritan	Bet Bullock	85
Jason Paul	Sheila Kelshaw	87
Goody Two-Shoes	Heather Norton	87
A Character	Minnie Douglas	88
Unrequited Love	Bet Bullock	89
Yasmin	Jean Allen	94
Time	Barbara Thackeray	98
A True Story	Minnie Douglas	99
A Sporting Dream	Dave Lightfoot	100
Snowdrops	Jean Allen	102
Gallant Galanthus	Jean Allen	103
Saints And Sinners	Bet Bullock	104
Old Age	Frank Hooley	105
Spice Girls	Frank Hooley	106
Memories	Jean Allen	107
A Disastrous Weekend	Win Francis	117
Nowhere To Go	Minnie Douglas	121
Aunt Ada's Visit	Bet Bullock	123
Second Parting	Bet Bullock	128
In the Garden	Jean Allen	130
Worlds Apart	Jean Allen	131
The Pin	Irene Ward	132
The Master Craftsman	Jean Allen	133
Love	Win Francis	134
Flight	Win Francis	135
Just an Ordinary Family	Becky Bollet	136
A Letter from Hospital to her Writer's Workshop Classmates	Irene Pryor	139
No Flies on our Bread Cakes Last Term	Irene Pryor	140
Friendship	Barbara Thackeray	144

Lowedges
Bet Bullock

I live on an estate called Lowedges
where care and concern know no measures.
Most people I've met
surpass any you'll get –
one or two should be national treasures.

Lowedges is a Pineapple
Roisin Birks

From the outside it's prickly and spiky

Before I worked in Lowedges all I knew of the estate was that it had a bad reputation. The estate has been tainted by the press with consistent negativity and a lack of forgiveness.

Inside it's an array of goodness

Over the last four years as a community worker here, my experience of Lowedges as a community worker includes an enthusiastic community spirit from young and old, a passion and desire to change and prove public opinion wrong.

Lowedges is a pineapple

From the outside it's prickly and spiky

Inside it's an array of goodness

Fuchsia Land
Jean Allen

Take a walk with me in the Fuchsia Land garden.

Angela Rippon is there at the front, trying to be noticed, but unfortunately, she's standing next to the *Wild and Beautiful Wicked Queen*. That is an unkind *Twist of Fate*. She wants to be by *Tom Thumb* as he is small and insignificant, or *Grandma Hobbs*, as she is old and comfortable.

Zeigfield Girl, at the other side of the garden, is flirting with *Rambo* and dying to get an invite to the *Grand Prix*. He seems more interested in *Naughty Nicole* who is sucking a piece of *Coconut Ice*. *Grumpy* sits in his corner, contemplating *Voodoo* in an effort to get rid of some of his rivals. *Caesar, Brutus* and the *Duke of Wellington* are his present bugbears. Last week it was *Winston Churchill* and *King George V*. *Cheeky Chantelle* threatened to tell his *Dark Secret*. He often thought he would like to get to know *Nell Gwyn* or *Madame Butterfly*. They had class. The only one who showed him any deference was *Mary Poppins* and she was a bit too *Flash* for his liking. At the bottom of the garden *Zulu King* did a *War Dance*, complete with *War Paint*. *Alice Sweetapple, Rosy Ruffles* and *Mrs. Popple* looked scared and offered him a *Danish Pastry* but he said he'd make them walk on *Hot Coals* for their *Impudence*.

"They should send him to *Crinkly Bottom* and make him live on *Orange Drops*," said *Hiawatha* as he dodged the *Friendly Fire* coming from the direction of *Uncle Charlie*.

"Someone ought to send him to the *University of Liverpool*," muttered *Robin Hood* who was practicing the *Highland Pipes* and wishing he could change his *Lincoln Green* for a nice *Red Jacket*.

The *Grand Duchess* and the *King of Hearts* looked magnificent in their pots, eating *Jam Roll* and *Scarborough Rock*. *Pussy Cat* was up to *Mischief*, chasing *Rooster* by

Torchlight. ***Lucy Locket*** played the ***Moonlight Sonata*** while ***Torville and Dean*** skated on a ***Chessboard***.

Alfie and ***Abigail*** discussed plans to go to ***Alaska*** as ***Tolling Bell*** heralded ***Evensong*** at the old church in ***Hathersage***. She wanted to go on the ***Orient Express***, eat ***Strawberry Mousse***, wear a ***String of Pearls*** and dance the ***Tennessee Waltz***.

The ***Gipsy Princess***, a ***Carioca*** at heart, longed for an ***Ocean Beach*** and ***Peppermint Candy***. "***Pinch Me***," she said, as she woke up from a lovely dream in which she had ***Blue Eyes***, wore a ***Blue Petticoat***, and ***Lord Jim*** and ***Rufus the Red*** were vying for her attention. When she realised it was only a dream, she cried ***Frozen Tears***. ***Goody Goody*** tried to comfort her and gave her a ***Silver Dollar***. Meanwhile ***Countdown Carol*** decided to join ***Green Peace*** and become a ***Trail Blazer***. ***Little Orphan Annie*** thought she might as well go along but it was ***Midwinter***; they could run into a ***Snowstorm***.

"The ***Six Squadron*** will have to form a ***Task Force*** to rescue us," said ***Carol***, " and I could wear my new ***Sarong***."

Westminster Chimes heralded the arrival of the ***Intercity***.

"***This England***," thought ***Sir Matt Busby***, "it's all ***Wine and Roses***." Then he went into the estate agents and planned next year's holiday on ***Vesuvius*** with ***My Mum*** and a ***Hawaiian Princess***.

Prayer

Jean Allen

Om mani padme om. Om mani padme om
drones like a million swarming bees,
paper wheels spin in Himalayan breeze
jewel hearted lotus, begging bowls and saffron robes.
Kneeling in the dust, foreheads on the ground
silence shattered by the call
that penetrates each whitewashed wall
and causes evening's shimmering heat to tremble in the blast.
Incense, smoking candles, tombs in ornate stone
haloed figures, coloured glass
rich gowned priests intoning Mass,
sighs and whispers fly from hearts of those assembled there.
A nagging fear of judgement, need for aid
in case, one day, a debt has to be paid.

Morning in Lowedges
Jean Allen

The moon, just a curved sliver of silver, faded as the inky black of the night slowly gave way to the lighter greys of dawn. Stars flickered and went out one by one as though some heavenly caretaker was tiptoeing through the skies snuffing out hundreds of twinkling lamps. As if at a signal, the sun began its majestic ascent, shooting out pale golden rays to announce its arrival as it climbed. Shadows flitted across quiet gardens like nightime ghosts hurrying to find shelter from the day. Birds fluttered with excitement, calling, singing and whistling to each other and the waking world.

A white cat squeezed itself out of a small upstairs window and landed with a soft plop on the sloping porch roof. It abseiled down the wall onto the cool drive, eyes black slits as it sat and smoothed its ruffled fur. Bow shaped whiskers twitched and the slits became wider as a sleepy spider began a zig-zag morning stroll to the front door. A flash of white lightening and the spider was swallowed into oblivion. The cat licked his lips and resumed washing, watching and waiting.

A smell of coffee and frying bacon seeped through the walls of a house. Noises distracted the vigilant cat: a door opening and closing, footsteps across the tarmac, a garage door scraping and the splutter and cough of a reluctant car engine as it was forced to leave its shelter and confront another day.

In small bedrooms, children buried themselves in cotton quilts, holding off the moment when warm skin would erupt in goose pimples as the cold air accosted it on the dash to the bathroom. School uniforms lay draped across chairs. Toys sat where they had been abandoned the night before.

A dog barked and strutted into the cul-de-sac to lay claim to his territory. The cat leapt up onto the porch roof and sat on the narrow windowsill above, looking down in annoyance and disdain. The silence was over; soon voices would be heard, some soft, some loud, some happy, some angry as the people of the cul-de-sac rose to meet whatever the day held for them.

Early Lowedges Recollections
Win Francis

I knew this area of Sheffield from my teens, as I camped with the Woodcraft Folk at Bennett's Farm in Dronfield Woodhouse most Sundays during the summers of the forties. In fact, my husband and I first met at these camps, so the place has a special significance for us.

When we had the opportunity to exchange council houses with the Lawfords and leave Shiregreen for Greenhill/Bradway, as it was originally known, we jumped at the chance.

We moved to Atlantic Road on a damp cold day in February 1957 in the back of a Co-op removal van containing our worldly possessions. The boys' pet goldfish only just survived the journey with about two inches of water remaining in their bowl. We were met by a building site and a sea of mud, but also by a tray of tea and biscuits from a kindly neighbour, intent on making us welcome in a gesture that epitomised the friendship we have enjoyed over subsequent years.

Our sons were six-and-a-half and eight years old and their first experience of our new home was to contract German Measles – a legacy from the Lawfords' children. Fortunately, it wasn't serious and they were soon able to start school at Bradway County School on Lowedges Road, where they wore the maroon blazer and cap that was the school uniform. They soon made friends with other children at the school and in the cul-de-sac, and I likewise with my neighbours. As luck would have it, an old school friend and her husband and two girls moved into the next block shortly after us, so we resumed our friendship.

The terminus shops were still under construction so we had to go to Bocking Lane for our groceries, which was quite a trek as the path and the parkway were not built. In fact, during the winter it was a quagmire of ponds and springs, with trees and shrubs scattered about. During the spring, it was a haven for frogs and tadpoles, which the boys brought home in jars.

A boon for housewives and the children was Alsop's mobile shop, an old blue single-decker bus which came round the estate on Friday evenings. But the boys enjoyed going to the Co-op at Bocking Lane, as they were fascinated by the system of wires and pulleys which took your money up to the raised office in the corner, and sent back your change to the assistant at the counter.

Soon after we moved in we were canvassed by Frank Hooley, who later became MP for Heeley, and we joined the Labour Party. This kept us very active and busy on the Estate – even the boys helped to deliver election literature each year.

Next winter we had a very heavy snowfall, settling so deep that the children could not get to school and my husband had to turn back after struggling to Woodseats – unable to go any further. It lasted for quite some time, and everyone had to dig their way out to the main roads, where the snowploughs cleared the bus routes.

I can't recall the date when the local authority called a meeting and several of us agreed to start a Tenants Association on the estate. We canvassed for members, and endeavoured to establish what people wanted from the association. We met at the Michael Church Hall – before the church was built – and this was the forerunner of the present Tenants and Residents Association. It was to be quite a few years though before we got the meeting hall that we campaigned for from the outset.

The boys derived much pleasure from watching the building of Reney Avenue, and then the thirteen storey flats on Atlantic Rd and Gervase Avenue. The number twenty-two bus came through Greenhill village and along Reney Avenue, going to Holmesfield via Tinkers Corner. We would often take that bus during the summer and walk down to Millthorpe and Cordwell Valley, where we would picnic and play in the stream. Autumn found us blackberrying in the hedges and looking for conkers.

Another favourite walk was over Totley Tunnel and on to Carr Lane, passing our old campsite. The boys loved to hear tales of our exploits in our younger days there.

Bradway was still mostly fields, and the boys loved to play cowboys and Indians up and down its hills and round the gorse bushes. We would hear the yellowhammers calling, "Little bit of bread and no cheese," and often surprised rabbits grazing on the grassy banks. Our younger son loved making models, and had his own miniature village in our back garden, with tiny balsa wood swings, a fountain and a model railway. Kids from round about stopped to look whenever they passed, and one recent postman told me he used to persuade his mum to go home from the shops that way so he could stop and look.

Before Greenhill library was opened we had a temporary library in one of the shop premises near the Magpie, but its size inevitably meant that there was no great choice of books. Being avid readers, we preferred to go to Woodseats library, which had, and still has, a wide variety.

As we saw the estate completed and the Greenhill Parkway built, it settled into maturity. Neighbours came and went, though some have remained. We saw the point blocks built and we saw them demolished. Our sons grew up and left home, as children do, but after nearly fifty years I think we shall settle where we are.

Gateshead
Barbara Thackeray

Life was anything but luxurious on Park Lane in Gateshead, the little town across the River Tyne from Newcastle where I was born in 1926.

All who lived there were very much in the same boat. However, they were good neighbours, rallying round if help was ever needed. Many of them acted as midwives for each other, which may seem shocking by today's standards, but of course we didn't have the Health Service as we know it today.

The houses were mostly two-up, two-down. Looking back makes me wonder how people brought up their families in such cramped conditions.

The two bedrooms were upstairs. My three brothers shared the largest. Among other things, it contained a double bed and a single. It was never a tidy place. The boys used to make aeroplanes out of newspapers. All you could hear from within were shrieks of laughter and weird noises, which presumably were meant to sound like aircraft engines.

My parents' bedroom was furnished with a full bedroom suite. I emphasise that only because it was something to be proud of in those days, when money wasn't easy to come by. Much effort went into furniture making. It was a highly skilled craft during that period and quality was good. Much of it is still around today. Furniture produced at the present time has nothing to compare, lots of it coming in flat packs. Mum took extra special care of hers; it must have taken a long time to save for, and probably meant doing without many other things in the process.

I never liked the smell of the geranium she had in the bedroom. It was not a particularly sweet smelling plant, but it was one of mum's favourites and definitely there to stay.

My sleeping area was downstairs. In our little sitting room we had a tall cabinet. Tucked inside was my foldaway bed. It was pulled out for me every evening, and hidden away again in the morning. It wasn't like having a bedroom of my own, but space was limited and it was the only solution.

I loved reading in bed and still do to this day. Not having any books of my own, I'd joined the library. I used to borrow books with stories about school buildings with secret passages, churches with ghostly figures, in fact any mystery tales were favourites with me. I hasten to add that my taste has changed somewhat since then.

There was no electricity in the house at all. The only lighting there was for me to read by was a gas lamp on the wall. Mum used to light it for me very carefully, as the gas mantle could easily be broken. I usually fell asleep whilst reading and she must have popped in then to put out the light.

When we were home from school on Saturdays, we used to hear a voice shouting in the street: "Any old rags!" It was the ragman, as we called him. If we had any, he would give us a balloon or a goldfish in a jar. He had a three-wheeled handcart which he pushed himself, although some were lucky enough to have a horse to do that for them.

Many times during the week we would wake up to the delicious smell of Mum's home baking, bread and pastries. We couldn't wait to taste them. She liked to make an early start to the day; there was plenty to do with four children to care for. Baking as much as she could herself was one way of ensuring that money was well spent.

A coal fire heated the oven. At the bottom of our road was a depot where we bought our fuel. The mountains of coal were piled high. Goods trains ran alongside making the deliveries. Jimmy, the man in charge, would deliver it for you for a small charge, otherwise you could collect it yourself, taking a small amount at a time. It was dirty stuff, but Mum had a pair of tongs which she used to put it on the fire.

It wasn't unusual to hear the clippity-clop of horses' hooves on the cobbled street. They were a common means of transport. A horse and dray were used to deliver barrels of beer to the pub across the road. They were rolled down a sloping board, into the cellar. Dad always said beer tasted better from a barrel than a bottle.

Bath time was a major event at our house. Out came the tin bath with handles at both ends. There was no hot water on tap, but Mum had managed to get a gas boiler to heat the water. She would pour in a little liquid Dettol, which smelt more like disinfectant than perfume. Dad usually got the job of emptying the bath, drying it out and hanging it on a hook in the back yard.

This area was shared with our neighbour. There were two toilets, one for each family. It's hard to imagine now what it was like to go to an outside toilet in the middle of winter.

Maried women didn't go out to work so much then. There were not so many career women. Some did little cleaning jobs. Housework was hard. No mod-cons in those days. Monday was the main washday for us, with another later in the week. The clothes were put into a tub of hot water and rubbed on a board, (a corrugated sheet of metal on a wooden framework, which stood inside the tub.) The white washing was then put into a boiler for half an hour or so. I remember the smell of the carbolic soap Mum used on collars and cuffs. When the washing was well rinsed they were put through a wringer. It had two rollers with a handle at one side which was used to turn them. A bucket or bowl was placed underneath to catch the surplus water.

Billy Smith's corner shop was a little gold mine. He stocked everything imaginable, there being no supermarkets. On the whole, people did their shopping daily. There were plenty of shops and the main High Street was only minutes away.

No one I knew had a refrigerator, therefore food couldn't be stored for long, hence the daily shopping.

Oranges were delivered to Billy's shop in long wooden boxes. They were securely tied with ropes, which he always saved for us. They made excellent skipping ropes and stretched right across the road. Lots of us played together, but we had to move when any mode of transport passed by.

Gas lamps lit the streets. We used to tie our ropes around them and make a swing, but if a bobby came within sight, we would grab the rope and run.

I remember the Walls ice cream man who used to visit our area regularly. He rode on a large tricycle with a white box fastened securely on to it. He would ring the bell on his trike loudly to let us know he was around. Most of the children, myself included, used to like the ice lollies. They weren't on a stick as today, but were in a small, triangular carton.

Although there weren't any green areas around Park Lane, we found all we needed at the local park. It was truly a very pleasant area, particularly during the spring and summer months, when the flowers were in full bloom.

As a treat, mum used to take us to the picture house (cinema) once a week, usually on a Monday, early evening. We would call at the sweet shop close by, and were allowed a choice, providing it was within the budget. Mum never had a problem with what she would have: always her favourite Liquorice Allsorts.

On a Saturday afternoon, my brothers and I used to get a penny from dad. We went to the same picture house to see the next episode of Flash Gordon. It was something we looked forward to, because each instalment ended at a most exciting point, which meant we had to wait a whole week to see how Flash got out of his latest predicament.

About two years before the outbreak of World War II, we were told that all the houses on Park Lane were to be demolished. We were moved to a new housing estate. While it was good to have a bathroom and gardens and the smell of newly mown grass, there just wasn't the atmosphere of Park Lane.

We missed the sound of the horses' hooves on the cobbled roads, the ragman's call, Billy Smith's corner shop, Jimmy's coal yard, and Dad missed the pub across the road.

I guess it's a case of: what you gain on the swings, you lose on the roundabouts.

The Key
Minnie Douglas

When I was twenty-four I was fortunate to be given the key to a brand new house. When I first went to see it with my husband, it was a cold, blustery day. The ground was sludgy and there were no roads. Houses were still being built all around. The thrill of putting the key in my own front door was something I cannot describe.

The walls were painted gray. We were told it would be six months before we could put wallpaper on them. I couldn't wait to move in to number twenty-three Gervase Drive, Lowedges.

I feel that was when my life began. There was one school called Greenhill. To get to it was a road, aptly named Atlantic. Everyone wore wellingtons. It was windy, wet and you had to wrap up warmly to attempt it. All the front gardens had to have lawns. Fancy flowerbeds and privet hedges were not allowed. I must say, when everyone cut their lawns, they did look good.

There were no shops, and no pubs at first, only a wooden hut selling sweets and papers. Eventually a school was built on the estate, a pub called The Magpie, and a row of shops.

My children were happy. Neighbours helped one another. We were all good friends, everyone, more or less, in the same age group. Along came more children, seven altogether, but with bunk beds, we managed to sleep everyone. All this took place fifty years ago.

Gone But Not Forgotten
Sue Roberts

Around the year 1956, two new estates were being built – Gleadless Valley and Greenhill. Greenhill later was changed to Lowedges.

What a joy to get the key to a brand new property – house, maisonette or flat - the smell of new timber and plaster, to have an inside toilet and bathroom, a far cry from the old tin bathtub beside the fire on a Friday night.

Some new residents had a small garden attached to their property. The old houses, two-up and two-down, were dirty and dingy, at least the one I lived in was.

At first we had few amenities. There were only two shops, one at each end of the estate. The Newsagents was called Ditchfield's. Vans used to come round daily with fruit and vegetables, bread and milk. You could get fresh fish once a week. Nobody felt the inconvenience because they all had new accommodation. Other shops opened quickly. The chemist was first, then the draper's. You could lay wool away and fetch it as you needed it, a couple of ounces at a time. In those days, many women still knitted their children's clothes. The draper's also sold plimsolls, wellingtons, shoes, slippers and sewing materials. The shop was called Stringfellow's. I worked there many years ago. Next came the fruit shop and butcher's, followed by a library that later became a wallpaper and paint shop - Gower's and Burgeon's General Store. Then came the Co-op and Post Office.

Lowedges School was one of the first buildings to be completed, and across the road St. Michael's Hall was built. They used to put shows on. Before he became famous, Joe Cocker sang there. The hall had a stage with a curtain so it looked right for a show. Later on, a new part was added adjoining the hall so that marriages, christenings and funeral services could be performed there. Many classes were held in the hall – karate, keep fit, slimming and dancing classes. We also went there to vote.

The first pub was The Magpie. They had many talent nights and it was at one of these nights that Marti Caine sang. I don't know if she won the competition, but she went on to do greater things and became a big star. She once lived on the estate, near the terminus. When Brocklehurst's, the garage, opened at Meadowhead, Diana Dors did the honours. They say she looked stunning and beautiful. I wouldn't have thought that for a moment! In 1958, Kirkhill Residential Home was opened by Queen Elizabeth, the Queen Mother. She was wearing a blue dress and coat with a matching hat. Nearly all the estate came out to see and cheer her.

For many years, flowers were planted in the middle of the road and outside the shops. They stayed there from one season to another.

A Youth Centre was opened and is still going strong, thanks to a group of people who give their time and effort to see that the children enjoy themselves. Next door is the Tennant's Hall. It is the grown-ups who enjoy themselves there, with Saturday Dances and Bingo every Monday, Wednesday and Friday.

The park, years ago, had everything: a café, tennis courts, golf, bowling greens, and at the far end, a children's play area with swings, slide, roundabout and small sand pit. There was a pavillion where children playing matches could change their clothes and have a cup of tea at half time. The park was a safe haven in those days, but sadly, no more. The café is always closed, and cricket no longer played. The bowling greens are kept in impeccable condition and children have planted flowers to try and bring the park back to how it used to look. It is the shops that look lost. Flowers have been replaced by stones set in concrete. Shutters have been put on all the windows and the shutters are covered in graffiti. But out of the darkness, there is light. Quite a few people are trying to get the community together again. At the Forum, there are classes to suit everyone – creative writing, computer studies, art and crafts. Agewell is for senior citizens who meet every Tuesday for interesting talks on many subjuects. There are musical mornings, including a chat and a cup of tea.

It is a high mountain to climb to get Lowedges like it used to be, but with hard work, perseverance and determination, I think it can be done.

Drugs
Irene Ward

He sat, an old ragged coat protecting him from the cold, hard pavement
his hair matted and dirty, oblivious to everything around him except for the sound
of the coins that now and again would drop into the can beside him.
His mangy, thin dog, a bowl of water at its feet, sat loyally by his side.
I tried to look away to save myself the sadness, but as I was passing
the boy lifted his head and I found myself staring into a pair of dark
stony eyes, not those of a boy of seventeen or so, but old eyes
weary and cold, without any life in their depth. My heart ached
as I thought to myself, why wasn't this boy chasing around
kicking a football on a fresh green field, eyes young and bright, full of life?

Home
Pat Bestall

My home is Lowedges. It's the capitol of Sheffield to me, like London is the capitol of England. We have attractions, like Lowedges Park. It is the same to me as London's Regent's park.

Our local shops are like Harrods on a smaller scale. Our fifty-three bus service is like the tube, overflowing with passengers getting from the terminus to the shops on the end.

The Learning Wing is our version of Eton, with brains doing overtime, and people nipping out for a fag when the going gets tough.

On the street corners are youths with bottles of alcohol in their hands, young girls with babies in prams, or still in their small, immature bodies, waiting to be born to the next unknown boy.

Drugs change hands and crimes take place, just like in London, but not highlighted as much. Our local fish and chip shop is our kind of Harry Ramsden's; the owner is even called Harry!

The terminus café is our one-stop centre, where we can always depend on a listening ear, a good cheap meal, bargain second-hand clothes and a laugh when feeling down. London's kind of Samaritans and soup kitchens all in one place.

Wreck-Tangle
Dave Lightfoot

Hello. My name is the Doctor – well, that's my nickname. I'd like to introduce you to some of my patients by writing a little story about their daily lifestyles. The majority of my patients are homeless street drinkers. The ones who are lucky enough to have their own flats or bedsits generally use them like hostels for their homeless friends. By the way, I'm not a doctor, I'm an ex-drinker, but still a friend, having spent many a year drinking on the streets in summer and at several flats in the winter, before the occupants were evicted because rent money turned into drink money.

On an average day, when it's starting to get light in the morning the flat is probably crowded. First things first – toilet, before there's a queue. I gently step over the sleeping bodies, trying not to make a noise, and then have a scout round for a live wire or livener – that is, a drink – which nine times out of ten there is, in the bank that would have been stashed, especially if it was Suicidal Sunday morning, when the offy opens at ten instead of eight, and nobody gets weighed in (to the Post Office) for beer tokens.

So, more often than not, it's off ham 'n' egging and the milk run drinks and dog ends outside pubs from the previous night. It's off up Ecclesall Road to the 24 hour SP Shop next to Endcliffe Park, where you could get a few good drops from people going for their Sunday papers or going to and from church. The people who I associated with were the Old School, just drinkers, not drug users.

We work in shifts, sitting begging on a piece of cardboard with our faithful dogs, politely requesting "spare change please sir," or "spare change please madam", and wishing them a nice day as well. This only really takes place on Suicide Sunday, and the first £1 goes on dog food, which my dog Rizla eats out of the carrier bag, whilst sat on the sleeping bag. One of the look-out men stands, more than likely, twenty yards away at the bus stop looking nonchalant, watching out for Police as they sometimes move you on or there could be a warrants out and you could be crowed.

The look-out takes the dog across the road every half hour into the park for a walk and a chat with the rest of the crew, who'll be sitting on a bench, and asks one of them to change shifts with whoever was begging, or if the person is buzzing after a few good drops, he stays seated and the dog walker takes him some roll-ups and his or her Lucozade bottle back, topped up with cider. If the bottle's full, the first drop would go on the floor – one for the girls and boys; that is, a drink for the ones that have unfortunately left us.

Having decided we've made enough, we call it a day. We do a bit of shopping on the way back to the flat and have a chat and watch telly if there is one, with a drink of course. Then, if we need to, we go to a suitable location for the second half of begging – the evening session. It might sound, to some people, rude and cheeky, but that's first impression; having spoken to some of my friends, you would probably be more understanding, instead of jumping to conclusions.

If there is no need to go begging (which is usually just a couple of times a week), we stay in the flat and, if the drinks run low, two of the school nip out to the shop for supplies – whatever's needed. Having all woken up mid-morning and all having had our wash and a shave, we plan the rest of the day accordingly, and split up and go about our business in twos and threes, and all meet up on the wall later, which is situated near the offy at Hanover, Broomhall (Cost Cutter). This is convenient. There's a little nature reserve called Sunnybank where we go and drink in the daytime. It's private and out of sight, where nobody is offended, and we always leave it tidy as we found it. Some of the lads crash out in the afternoon for an hour: it's called gouching, especially if they'd had sherry and a spliff. It's like a creeper – it makes you tired, unless you pace yourself. It depends on the individual.

You sometimes get outsiders joining the school, and you can always get a greedy guzzler; that's why we share the drinks clockwise and whilst walking we regularly have a pit stop so we don't run out of petrol. We (the old school that is) always pride ourselves, if you can call it that, on being polite and friendly at all times, and not offending the public. If somebody seems to be a bit the worse for wear, he or she would be encouraged to go back to the cesspit and instructed to let the rest in later using a certain code, i.e. knocking in a certain way; plus, we'd be bearing gifts.

Going back to the morning's activities I started to talk about earlier, as we are eventually all awakened by the noise of the toilet, or more likely the opening of drinks, we start our daily chin-wag, talking about all sorts of all our yesterdays and, yes, the majority of drinkers all have nicknames. The school is always unpredictable. Drinkers come and go during the morning, depending on their state and commitments – if they have any.

No two days are the same, and we all know where to find each other by the knowledge and experience of days gone by – Cathedral, Peace Gardens, bottom of the Moor, etc. There are also more private drinking holes where you don't have an audience. We're all here: Pond St. Nora, Subway Cyril, Quick Fit Fitter (Alcoholics' fits), Soft Porn Sean, Rant and Rave Dave, Bat & Ball Paul, German Helmet, Fartin' Martin, Aunt Sally, Johnny Bogroll, Tweety Pie, Night & Day, Ray the Hat – and many more.

The Terminus Cafe
Diary of a Corner Shop
Jean Allen

2001

I've had what some might call an eventful life. At one time, I sold cards, a pleasant enough occupation, but many will remember me as the old butcher's shop. I've always done my best to make people feel welcome when they come to visit. However, in 2001, I went through a very bad patch. No one seemed to want me anymore. Left alone and empty, I was at my lowest ebb. Then suddenly some people began studying me. I had a pretty neglected look by this time. You get that way when nobody cares about you. Anyway, God had something to do with it apparently. It turned out they were His friends. I didn't know anything about Him, but I was willing to accept any help I could get and if He could change things for me, then I'd be very happy.

September: People started coming in and discussing a makeover of all things! That didn't sound like a bad idea, though some of the changes they proposed seemed a bit drastic. I knew there was room for improvement, but hey, lets not rush things! They couldn't make up their minds what I should become – a coffee shop for older folk? (that sounded O.K.); – a drop in centre for everyone? – (well..., maybe); a place for young people? (Oh, I don't know about that. They'd have to behave themselves. Mind you, if God thinks it's alright, that's fine. He's the boss.)

My owners really wanted these church folk to have me. Other people got involved – Lowedges Community and Safety Forum, the Regeneration Officer, Lowedges Crime and Disorder Partnership. It was all a bit overwhelming. I heard mutterings about the Terminus being a trouble spot – bad reputation and all that. Well that's not my fault is it? I'm stuck here and I can't move. There are a lot of good people around too, I know, I've heard them talking. Anyway, it was agreed that it might not be a bad idea to use me, and the next thing I knew, this group of ministers came to me for a meeting. I could see they were excited. I was too.

2002

January: They were discussing my makeover again. Some officials came snooping round. They gave me a thorough going over, didn't miss a thing and wrote it all down. They kept shaking their heads and tut-tutting and the next thing I heard was that it would take fifty thousand pounds to get me properly into shape. Is that a lot? They seemed to think so.

February: It looked as though I was about to be abandoned again. The church folk told my owners they didn't have the money. I thought God was sponsoring all this. I'd heard them saying that He could do anything. In fact, He'd told them himself, "Nothing is impossible to Me." If that's the case, I really can't see a problem. Anyway, I wasn't the only one getting upset. The people at the Forum Meeting got mad too. They wanted me to get my makeover and be useful again. They seemed to have the idea I would make a difference to the bad behaviour around here if the church folk got me. I'm not quite sure what they thought I could do, but they ended up sending the church folk off to "go and tell God the problem!" I quite agreed.

February 8th: There was no news from the church group. Then, I heard that another prospective tenant was coming to look me over. Those were roller coaster days. I felt nervous as I waited patiently. No one came.

February 14th: The church group were back. They seemed to be making definite plans for my makeover, but, as usual, money came into it. To make a start, they needed seventy pounds a week, plus my heating and lighting. Well, I can't do without that, can I? They looked a bit down in the mouth. I really don't understand them. I distinctly heard them say once that God had told them, "I own the silver, I own the gold," and "All creation and its bounty are mine... call for help when you're in trouble – I'll help you." They must have short memories.

February 15th: They're funny people. They got wildly excited because one of their elderly church members promised to give five pounds a week. It sounded a long way off seventy pounds plus, and didn't come anywhere near fifty thousand. Anyway, it was a start. Then they decided it was all too risky and they'd better see if they could find a cheaper place. Oh dear, I feel very confused about God's way of doing things.

February 20th: Someone else became interested in me. My owners were getting anxious. They really did want the church group to have me, but with another prospective tenant showing up, they told them they would have to make up their minds that very afternoon if they really wanted me. I was so nervous my windows rattled. Everybody seemed to be talking about me. I felt quite important. I hoped God would persuade them to have me. They seem to have a bit of difficulty communicating with Him at times. Then it happened – finally, a decision! They agreed to lease me for three months. That didn't give me a great sense of security! I'd hoped it would be for longer. I really didn't want to have to go through this again. In the end, February turned out to be quite a month. Two people at Greenhill Methodists each gave one hundred pounds after morning service. Next day they got one hundred and forty pounds from The Bridge Cafe at Totley. So – the first month's rent was in. That was good but I can't help thinking God has a tendency to leave things to the last minute.

March: I have to take back what I've just written. They got two gifts of one thousand pounds, so three months rent was in with some to spare. They decided I should sell second hand goods, drinks and biscuits. I would have liked something a bit more up market, but my opinion wasn't asked. I would only be opening on Wednesdays, Thursdays and Fridays. Such a shame, I feel I have a lot more to offer. The good thing was that people from all over the estate and beyond volunteered to help look after me.

April 18th: My big day: the opening! My windows sparkled as I showed off all the goodies I'd been given. The little lilac teapot I'd grown quite fond of was the first to be sold. I'd noticed a lady looking at it days before. In fact everything seemed to be disappearing. I was worried in case they didn't have replacements. It would have been so humiliating to have an empty window after all the fuss; after all, that's what gets people in. I couldn't help thinking it was a bit of a hand-to-mouth existence, but one of their friends said, "If it's God's hand and my mouth, I'll have everything I need."

June/July: I actually got a celebrity visiting me – Meg Munn, she's a politician, whatever that means. Anyway, it's important I think. Then Joy, one of the ministers, talked about me on the radio so lots of folk know about me now.

August: I got all steamed up when they had the 'Share Jesus' week. They had to keep the door open to give me some air. Over 50 youngsters visited me. I got knocked about a bit when they kept crowding in, but they weren't bad really.

Christmas: Carols and mince pies. I was very popular. They'd made a special effort to make me look nice, which I appreciated.

2003

January: They agreed to lease me for 5 years with no rent increase, as long as my wiring got fixed. Sounds like major surgery, but, needs must, and they said I'd feel better when it was done.

April 18th: My first birthday as God's Cafe. (That's how I like to think of myself now I know a bit more about Him.) It was Easter. I had a lovely display of the garden tomb in my window. It even made one resident cry. He hadn't expected ever to see anything like that on Lowedges. To be honest, I felt sad, too, when I heard how they'd killed God's Son a long time ago, though apparently, He didn't hold it against them, simply brought Jesus back to life. He's very much alive now because his next move was to get us serving hot food! I was given a Neighbourhood Renewal Grant and that paid for my fridge, freezer and microwave. Meg Munn was back again and she brought the Lord Mayor with her this time.

August: Councillor Keith Hill came to me for a meeting with residents and shop keepers to discuss the bad behaviour of some people. As a result, they actually made some changes to reduce crime here at the terminus. I do love eavesdropping on their meetings. Guess what? Two thousand pounds from the Tenants and Residents Association came in so I could get my toilet spruced up. Not before time, I thought. I do like to look my best and it had been quite an embarrassment to me.

October: I'm becoming multi-skilled – I think that's the word for people who can do lots of things. I started hosting a "Worship at the Terminus" service each month. Anybody can come.

Christmas: Again! Carols and mince pies, the Lord Mayor; Keith Hill, and torrential rain, but I got my name in The Star!

Did I mention the young people? I wasn't too keen on having them at first. You feel a bit fragile as you get older. Anyway, they come on Tuesday evenings and seem to enjoy having someone to listen to them. I guess they have a lot of problems and my people try to help them to cope. All sorts of people visit me; foreigners who are missing their families, folk who are lonely or sad. I've been there myself, I know what it's like to have a hard life. Perhaps God can help them like he helped me. Anyone can stick a little message on my Prayer Board, then my folk ask God to help them. My guess is that God knows all about them anyway, but likes having a chat with his friends and really does enjoy making things better for people. Another thing I think I do rather well is pass on information. I'm very well informed about many subjects – oh dear, I sound as though I'm boasting and God's not keen on that, but you should see all my posters!

They've lots of plans for my future. I've never had so many friends. I've come to the conclusion that they're right about

God. An old friend of theirs called Paul, who I haven't met yet, wrote to them, "God can do anything, you know – far more than you could ever imagine or guess or request in your wildest dreams!"

Daffodil

Win Francis

She breaks through the cold hard earth with her pale green stalk, defying winter to linger much longer.

She reaches towards the sky, standing straight and tall, nodding her head in the wind but remaining unbowed. Her yellow bud, clothed in its fragile sheath, gives little indication of the splendour of her maturity. But what glory unfolds from its delicate cover; the proud golden trumpet surrounded by its ruff of paler petals, calling to Mother Nature to prepare for pleasanter days.

She is my harbinger of Spring, the daffodil, growing in profusion in my garden.

Faith
Barbara Thackeray

Oh that there may always be
rivers flowing down to sea
gardens glowing with colour and pride
birds nesting in springtime
their young by their side
squirrels hiding their nuts in the grass
scampering back to their tree house
till winter has passed
the sly cheeky fox slinking around
delight of the children
when there's snow on the ground
the wonder of the sky at night
the stars and the moon
emitting their light.
And when times are troubled
as they well can be
may we find comfort
in the knowledge that we
will be guided by God
throughout our pain
till a new dawn breaks
like sun after the rain.

Stuff Happens
Bet Bullock

Carol replaced the telephone receiver and stood staring into space.

'Who's Sandy?'

Startled, she turned round. Her husband was standing in the kitchen doorway.

'Oh! You made me jump. What are you doing home at this time?'

'Popped home to get changed, the chief's lumbered me with a job tonight. Who were you talking to?'

'You look in a bad mood. What's he dumped on you this time?'

'I am in a bad mood, so who the hell was that on the phone?'

Carol stared at him. Tall, dark and handsome, that's what had attracted her to him...had she ever really been in love with him? She couldn't remember.

'It was Sandra,' she replied, 'a friend from my university days. I told you about her months ago. We hadn't seen each other for years until she spotted me in the library. We've met several times since. She rang to ask had I heard it was the Old Girls' reunion next weekend.' She pushed past him and walked into the kitchen. 'Have you had any lunch? I haven't started dinner yet, but I could make you a sandwich if you like.'

Dennis turned and followed her. 'I don't remember you mentioning any Sandra or Sandy.'

'You were probably watching football and didn't listen to me, as usual.' She opened the refrigerator door. 'Cheese or cold beef?'

'Sod the bloody sandwich!' He leaned over her and slammed the door shut. The sudden movement trapped her hand in the handle, twisting her wrist.

She yelped and turned on him, nursing her arm. 'For goodness sake! What's the matter with you?' she said angrily. 'You could have broken my wrist.'

'It's that bloke you've been seeing, isn't it? Sandra my eye! You're quick-witted, I'll give you that.'

Carol sighed and shook her head. 'For the umpteenth time, I have not been going out with a bloke. What makes you think I have?'

'You've started going out nearly every night for a start.'

'So what? You're out 'til all hours. When you do come home you're either too tired to speak, or drunk. Usually both.'

'You know what my job's like, it's not nine to five. As for drinking, if I didn't unwind I'd go crazy. What gets me is you never tell me where you're going or where you've been. What am I to think?'

'Why do men always think it's another man? I've got friends you know, unlike you, who haven't any. You're to busy sucking up to your boss.'

She marched into the sitting room, opened a bureau drawer, pulled out a photo album and flicked through it. 'Come here and look at this,' she shouted.

Dennis joined her and she handed him the open album. 'Photos of a group of my university pals. The dark haired woman with her arm round my shoulders is Sandra, who prefers to be called Sandy. Satisfied?'

Dennis stared at the photographs, closed the album and dropped it on to the coffee table.

'It doesn't look like you! You've got blonde hair and you're not wearing glasses.'

'My hair's now as nature intended, mousy brown. Then, I wore contact lenses, but my eyes got itchy, okay? Anyway, never mind about me. That's Sandy, right?'

Dennis shrugged. 'If you say so. How the hell would I know? Huh! It could be anybody, it proves nothing.'

He walked over to a drinks cabinet and poured himself a large whisky.

Carol picked up the album and put it back in the drawer. 'So, you think I'm lying?'

Dennis plonked down on a settee. 'I've always thought of you as the only honest person I know. What you see is what you get. Recently, though, you've changed, you're remote. Cold and sarcastic. You're not the girl I married, that's for sure. Look, if it's not another bloke, what is it?'

Carol walked to the drinks cabinet and poured herself a large sherry. 'I won't be having many more of these.'

Dennis frowned. 'Why not? What are you on about now?'

Carol sat down in an armchair, folded her slim legs beneath her and put her glass on the table. 'I'm pregnant.'

Dennis jumped up spilling his drink. 'Pregnant! You're having a baby?'

'Well, I hope so. What do you think I'm having, a litter of kittens?'

'Oh very droll. See what I mean? You're sarky all the bloody time.'

He drank what remained of his drink, helped himself to another one and returned to the settee. 'Thought you were on the pill.'

'I stopped. I wanted a child.'

Dennis grinned. 'Ah, well now, that's great! I hope it's a boy.'

'What would you do if it were a girl? Trade her in for a boy at an orphanage?'

'Don't be daft.' He put his glass on the table, stood up and walked towards her. He perched on the arm of her chair, put his arm round her shoulders and kissed her. 'So, this is why you've been acting weird. Hormones playing you up.'

'No, no it isn't. I've only just found out.'

'Oh, right. Well, what is it then?'

Carol picked up her glass and sipped her sherry.

'Well?' said Dennis impatiently.

'Yes, okay. It's us.'

Dennis frowned. 'Us? What's wrong with us?'

'Our marriage doesn't work any more.'

Dennis removed his arm and stood up. 'Rubbish!'

'Oh, come off it Den, there are times we're like strangers sharing a house.'

'We've not stopped having sex.'

'That's what you think. Anyway, there's more to a marriage than that.'

Dennis returned to the settee and picked up his glass. With it halfway to his mouth he stopped. 'Just a minute! What do you mean that's what you think?'

'We've not had sex for three months, maybe longer.'

'Eh? Don't be daft! Of course we have.'

Carole sipped her sherry. 'How long do you think it's been then?'

'Well I suppose we don't have it as often as we used to. I'm so bloody tired, the damn job's making an old man of me. Hang on though. The other day you said we had.'

Carol put her glass on the table, uncurled her legs and sat forward in her chair. 'I lied.'

Dennis, about to lean back in his chair, sat bolt upright. 'Lied! What do you mean you lied?'

'Just that. You asked me if we'd got it on last night and I said yes. I lied, we hadn't.' She rose to her feet. 'Oh, for goodness sake! You've just said it. You're always dog-tired. You forgot to add the important bit, nearly always drunk. Anyway, sometimes you fumble about. And, on odd occasions, almost get to it, but you don't. You fall asleep or I gently push you away. Needless to say, you don't remember either.'

Dennis got to his feet and started pacing about. He stopped abruptly. 'Right! Well I'm not tired or drunk now, so let's get upstairs and get on with it. You won't push me away this time.'

Carole spread her arms out invitingly, 'Why don't we do it here?'

Dennis looked at the windows. 'Ah! Well, yes, I suppose we could draw the curtains.'

Carol laughed. 'Oh Den, you're priceless! Why have you never jumped on me for God's sake? Doesn't desire ever make you reckless? On the other hand, haven't you forgotten something?'

Carole patted her stomach.

'Oh Christ! Yes, you're pregnant.' Dennis flopped back on the settee then quickly sat up.

'Hang on, if what you're saying is true it means it can't be mine.'

'Correct, give the man a cigar.'

'But, but,' he spluttered, 'you said you haven't been going out with anybody. You said, once and for all, you're not going out with another man.'

'And I'm not.'

'Well, you must have been. Dennis looked puzzled, 'I don't get it. Have I missed something?'

'It's really quite simple,' said Carol patiently. 'I'd decided to leave you but wanted a child. Not yours, because you might have fought me for custody.'

'I bloody would!' he interrupted angrily.

'Exactly, so, along came a bloke who was willing and he obliged. We had to do it several times of course – '

'And obviously one of them bloody worked so spare me the details.' He rose again, his face contorted with anger. 'You might at least have waited to get pregnant until after you'd left me.'

'I couldn't, he works abroad and was only here on leave.'

'Do I know the bugger?'

'No.'

'You calculating bitch! You've been planning this for bloody months haven't you?'

'Yes,' she said sadly, 'I should never have married you in the first place, really. I'm sorry.'

He bunched his fists and stepped towards her. 'Sorry! Not half as bloody sorry as I am, I've a good mind to – '

Carol stood up and looked him straight in the eye. 'Thrash me? I don't think so. Whatever would your Chief Inspector say?

I know what he'd think, I deserved it, but he'd have to suspend you because, despite provocation, we can't have a detective sergeant in the Met who's a wife beater, now can we?'

'Clever bugger! I knew you'd had it away with somebody, I just knew.' He picked up the whisky bottle and carried it to the coffee table. He poured some in his glass and put it to his lips.

'Didn't you say you had to go out tonight?' said Carol sitting down again.

'Oh Christ! Well I'll just have to rustle up a driver. Might as well drink this as I've poured it.' He dropped on to the settee again and they sat in silence.

Carole finished her drink and stood up. 'If you don't want anything to eat I'll get myself something.'

Dennis grunted. 'You'd be better spending your time packing and be gone by the time I get back. You'll get no money out of me, y'know. And I'm not selling this house.'

'I don't want anything other than my personal property.'

'Where will you live then? You've no job and no money of your own.'

'I'm moving in with Sandy. She lives alone and has a big house. Her parents have gone to live in Spain.'

'She knows all about this, I suppose. Does she know the bloke you've been with?'

'Quite well, actually. It's her brother.'

'Bloody hell! Is that why she's taking you in?'

'No. We're in love with each other.'

'What, you and the brother?'

'No, Sandy and I.'

Dennis sagged back and looked at her in amazement. 'What! Jesus! She's a bloody dyke! And that means you – no, I can't believe – Christ! What can I tell –'

'Your precious governor?' Carole smiled. 'Not to worry. Tell him I've run off with the milkman and it's good riddance.'

The Mercenary
Jean Allen

Ken Williams, referred to as Kamikaze Ken by some who knew him, sat smoking in a tobacco-streaked hotel room in a rundown street in Paris. Dingy nets hung limply at the open window. Shrill street sounds occasionally pierced his thoughts. His surroundings no longer bothered him. Born in Yorkshire, he had joined the army at fifteen and stayed in until he was thirty-five. He'd then made the decision to use his training in more lucrative and exciting ways. Although danger was always a factor, the anticipation of a job was like a drug to Ken, and today there was a job coming up. He glanced at the telephone, willing it to ring. He would be sixty this year but had no thought of retirement. He expected that one day he would die in some unknown backwater, probably someplace most people had never heard of. There would be few, if any, to mourn him.

He lit another cigarette, feeling the tension building in his shoulders. The ticking of the clock on the rickety table that doubled as a bedside locker irritated him. He shoved it under the pillow but could still hear it. The phone rang. An hour later Ken was at the Charles de Gaulle airport, his only baggage a battered hold-all inside of which was crammed his basic survival kit.

Thousands of miles away, Alison Davison felt a ripple of anxiety run through her as she looked out on the misty African sunrise. The rains would start any time now, bringing cooler days. For years the beauty of this country, which she now called home, had thrilled her, but not today. She looked around at the rough mud and wattle houses. Her neighbours began to appear at their doors, but their usual happy chatter had been replaced by a tense silence. Even the children seemed subdued.

Alison's father had died when she was five. Not long afterwards her mother remarried a man in whose life children had no part. Aunt Maud had taken in the thin, mousy haired girl with mischievous eyes and determined mouth. Their years together had been happy. After teacher training college, she had come to Africa as a volunteer aid worker ten years ago. The warmth and vibrant life of the jungle was a magnet to Alison. At the end of her term of service, she had gone back to England and stayed just long enough to sell up. Aunt Maud had died, leaving her everything. Her only sadness, as she left for Africa again, was saying a final goodbye to the home that had filled her younger years with so much pleasure.

Today, she felt only apprehension as she waited for the truck bringing fellow Brits from the sawmill at Batswende. The insurrection was gaining momentum. Villages were being destroyed as rebels rampaged through the forest, leaving a trail of fear and confusion. Those who refused to join them were killed. Homes were burnt. Foreigners were prime targets, and as Alison returned the muted morning greetings of her neighbours, she knew that her presence only increased their danger. She had to leave and hope she could come back one day. She would travel with her friends to Kisangani where they could get a plane to Kinshasa and England. She was thirty-six now and knew it would be hard to adjust to life anywhere else.

A disturbance at the edge of the village drew her attention and soon a small group of villagers, supporting a tearful, exhausted boy, made their way to her. His eyes bulged with terror as he gasped out the news, news she could not have imagined in her worst nightmares. The rebels had reached Batswende. He had escaped the attack with just a handful of others from his village and had been sent to warn Alison. The truck would not be coming. All her friends were dead, murdered when rebels attacked their village and took over the sawmill. Many Africans had died too. She felt numb, and suddenly, very alone. The danger was much closer than she had thought and far worse. Bo Martin, black face shiny with perspiration and wrinkled with concern, stepped forward,

"Alison, let me take you to the Catholic Mission at Wanie

Rukula. If we leave now, we can get there by nightfall and you will be safer." She had met Father Wilhelm and his younger colleague, Father Christophe on several occasions. The nuns, Agnes and Delores, were trained nurses, both Americans. She had enjoyed the opportunity to speak English when she visited them, usually because of some medical emergency. She mentally checked her baggage. Only absolute necessities could be taken. What was left, her friends could share out. She could not burden Bo Martin with a heavy load when speed was essential and every hour with her put his life in danger.

They reached the Mission compound at dusk. Its white painted walls glowed softly as glaring sunlight was replaced by hazy shadow. She felt some of the tension drain away as they went through the gates. The tears she had been holding back all day felt like a dam waiting to burst. Sister Agnes ran out to greet them. Her face was pale, clothes crumpled. Her fear was almost tangible. All signs of the usual orderly cheerfulness had vanished. A band of rebels was less than a day's march away. The missionaries were packing what they could into their jeep before setting out at dawn for Kisangani. A quick prayer, then thanks and hugs mingled as Bo Martin set off into the darkness back to his village.

At the Mission, they sat through the night, talking, dozing. It was barely light when they squeezed into the jeep, finding spaces for themselves in between the piled up baggage. As they set off, the rumble of approaching rain signalled the end of the dry season. Soon it was coming down in torrents, beating on the jeep roof, making conversation impossible as they bounced along the trail. Each silently meditated on what might lie ahead of them. Alison thought about her murdered friends.

Ken Williams, on the plane from Paris, settled down as comfortably as he could. It was impossible to plan a strategy in these situations. He would do that when he met up with the others. A few hours sleep would be good. He closed his eyes and did not open them until the voice of the captain broke into his dreams, announcing that in fifteen minutes they would be landing in Kinshasa. It was raining there and the temperature was 97F, humidity 90%. Ken yawned, stretched and dragged his mind back to the mission ahead.

Sleep was impossible for Alison as Father Wilhelm struggled to keep the truck upright on the slippery track. Rivers that had been dry for months now threatened to become torrents. Log bridges spanning wider rivers were easily dislodged as hard earth became muddy swamp. There would be no repairs possible now until the rains finished.

The truck skidded, wobbled for a few seconds, then rolled gently onto its side in the undergrowth. They heaved and shoved, struggling to right it but without success. Soaked, cold and miserable, the anxious group tried to get their bearings. There was a village a few miles away. They set off, carrying what they could. The priests were known in the area and would be given shelter; then, perhaps the next day, with more helpers, they could get jeep back on the trail.

The sky was already shaking out its billowing purple evening gown as they approached their destination. The rain had stopped, leaving a waterlogged path which sucked their rubber flip flops off their feet at every step. Swirls of steamy air smouldered up from the ground, floating round them like wispy grey ghosts. People came quickly out of their houses to see who their visitors were. The usual warmth in the welcome was missing but the bedraggled party was offered shelter for the night. Some villagers talked openly about joining the rebels rather than risk the alternative. A few hours rest and some food were all that the travellers could hope for.

Nightfall came. Manioc, rice and fish made a welcome meal. One by one, the lights from the fires went out, conversations faded until only the voice of the forest singing its night time harmonies could be heard. Two men kept watch in case there was a surprise attack. As Alison settled down to sleep, she wondered whose side they were on.

Suddenly, noise erupted in the darkness. Dogs barked. People screamed. Sparks flew skywards as flames sent spears of yellow light curling up from burning huts. Shadowy figures ran about in confusion. Spears flashed. Knives slashed. Gunfire crackled. Chaos.

Alison found herself gripped by strong hands and half dragged, half pushed along the ground deeper into the forest.

"Don't speak," a voice whispered, and she recognised Sister Delores was with her. Of Sister Agnes and the two priests there was no sign. They had stayed in other homes and, she learned later, were the rebels' first victims.

Morning. They shivered in the cold mist, clutching their damp clothes to them as they crept back to the silent village. Smoking embers were all that remained of many huts. The rebels had gone. Shocked villagers emerged from the forest. The smell of burning clung to them as they prepared to bury the dead. As Alison and Sister Delores helped, they knew they now had no alternative but to try to reach Kisangani alone and on foot.

Next morning, they set out through the forest. A trail led to another village a day's walk away where they might find shelter. It had once been a flourishing little market town with its own airstrip but was now reduced to a few dilapidated huts. Half a dozen families eked out their existence, unwilling to break ties that had bound them to this place for generations. But who could two white women, alone in the middle of an African uprising, trust?

Ken Williams climbed into the twin engine sixteen-seater plane they had managed to charter when they reached Kisangani. His companions, Ginger Carstairs, Bryn Jones, and Rob McIlvoy had met him at Kinshasa and the commercial flight from there had given them time to formulate a plan. They had been on missions together before and worked well as a team. Their pilot, a wily old Frenchman living in Kisangani, had for some time had been dependent on charter flights. Regular runs had stopped as the uprising gathered momentum so he was glad of any work these days. This was one charter however that he had been reluctant to accept. It gave him a bad feeling. He'd demanded twice his normal fee and got it. Now, he taxied down the runway, his job to fly over the surrounding forest looking for foreigners – coffee growers, loggers, missionaries, medical people – anyone who might be heading for Kisangani to escape the rebels. He had already decided he would keep the engine running if they found a spot to land, and he would not be hanging around. Any sign of trouble, and his passengers were on their own. Their search would begin north of Batswende and from there they would make their way back, circling over the places where villages were located.

Hardened as these men were, the destruction they looked down on sickened them. Homes destroyed, bodies lying in the dirt while dogs scavenged around them. A brief stop at Batswende, where they talked to the few survivors, made their mission even more urgent and they were soon airborne again. They passed over the Catholic Mission where they had expected to find people. Landing in a field from which maize had recently been harvested, they soon discovered the place to be deserted. An hour's search of the area revealed no one and they could only hope this meant the missionaries had escaped. They would keep a sharp look out as they flew back but there were few places to set a plane down. When questioned, the pilot sulkily told them of an almost deserted town on the way to Kisangani which had once had an airstrip. They decided to land there and search. As they approached the place, they spotted through the tree tops a group of rebel soldiers an hour's walk away from the town and making in that direction. Anyone running from them was likely to be caught very soon.

The pilot was by now reluctant to land at all. The sweat dripping from his eyebrows was not purely due to the heat. His throat felt tight and his mouth dry. He rubbed a grubby cloth across his brow, trying to dry his wet hands at the same time. The sight of the rebels terrified him. However, his more immediate danger came from four white men each with a gun trained on him. They landed. The four set off in different directions, following a plan. Time was short, but if anyone was hiding, they would find them.

Ken had often wondered about these jobs. Initially, money had been the attraction but lately, although he never knew the people he was sent to help, the heady feeling he had when a mission was completed successfully was like nothing else he had ever experienced. He had to admit that this feeling probably meant more to him now than the money.

The two women watched the plane circling overhead and realised it must be going to land at the village. Where was it from and why was it here? Weapons for the rebels? Government forces? They had no means of knowing but decided that they would use every bit of strength they had to get there and find out. The rebels were close but, as yet, neither they nor the women were aware of the other's presence.

The blow came from behind. The women fell forward together. They struggled to turn and face their attackers. A quick glance at each other was all the comfort they had. Fear was the only emotion they were conscious of – icy cold and paralysing. The voice spoke sharply,

"Come on girls, get a move on. We've got a plane to catch and the pilot is jittery." The broad Yorkshire accent was like a bucket of cold water being thrown over them. Energy returned with a rush. The unshaven, crinkled face showed just an inkling of a smile as the speaker helped them up. "Sorry about the rough introduction but I didn't want you to run off or start screaming." His radio crackled as he advised his colleagues to return to the plane.

They set off at a steady trot, oblivious to the thorns that tore their skin as they pushed forward. Eyes down, they watched for roots and creepers that would trip them, or more dangerous creatures that lurked under leaves and in bushes. As the plane came in sight, they saw Ginger racing towards it. Bryn and Rob soon appeared, running across the field. The girls stumbled forward and were pushed into the plane. The pilot was already taxiing down the rough runway. Shots vibrated in the distance. In seconds the plane was rising. The men disentangled themselves from their equipment and grinned as the two women hugged each other and tried to find suitable words to thank their rescuers. They would be back at Kisangani in a couple of hours and from there to Kinshasa for a plane home.

***

Alison settled in Derbyshire, living in a small cottage and working as a farm hand. She never felt any inclination to contact her mother but she never lost touch with the mercenary. He was a wild man in many respects, but he had come into the jungle and saved her. Sometimes she would get a postcard with no message other than Hi Ali, and signed K – just a picture that told her where he was. She found herself waiting for them.

For several days, an insurrection in Afghanistan had been the top story on the news. Special troops had been sent in. Alison received a postcard. It was from Afghanistan. She tuned in to all the news broadcasts but, suddenly, it was over. The clipped, precise tones of the newscaster briefly mentioned that the attempted coup in Afghanistan had failed. There had been a few British casualties but the situation was now peaceful. It seemed this small event on a huge world stage was already forgotten but after that no more post cards came.

Alison gathered her books together and tidied the desks, which had been pushed into disarray as the students clattered out of class at the end of the day. She had been back in the village in Africa a year now. Sometimes it felt as though she had never been away and the three years in Derbyshire were fading like an old photograph. With some of her money, she had helped rebuild the village school. She walked outside and lingered by the small garden that surrounded the school on three sides. Sweet smelling herbs intermingled with multicoloured flowers. The whitewashed walls gleamed, reflecting the sun's brightness. She breathed in the warmth and scents of Africa and sighed with contentment as she looked up at the proud sign over the school door: The Ken Williams Academy of Learning. She would never forget the man who had come into the jungle and saved her. So it was that in one small spot in Africa the mercenary was immortalised. It was the only memorial he ever had and one more than he ever expected.

Rain
Bet Bullock

Clouds
whispering trees
and shoppers scurrying.
Anxious mothers jostling umbrellas
ceaseless torrents, impassable roads
swollen rivers and flooded fields.
Carrier of death.

Showers.
Blossom fragrance
and glinting jewelled webs.
Grateful gardeners, laughing lovers
crystal streams, golden corn
miracle of rainbow splendour.
Giver of life.

Love Poem
Bet Bullock

Sleep quiet, sleep well.
Remember
there is one in this brief span of time
who loves you more than any other.
Sleep quiet, sleep well
for even now
you are in loving arms embraced
and as you drift in dream
a sweet and gentle kiss will caress your cheek.

Valentine
Bet Bullock

I give you a postcard
of pounding sea on a rocky shore
like the beating of my heart
when you smile and touch my hand

I give you a postcard
of a glorious sunset filling the sky
like the feeling of warmth in my soul
when you look into my eyes

I give you a postcard
of towering snow-capped mountains
like the uplifting of my being
when you whisper in my ear

I give you a postcard
of a fat lady trying to sit on a deck chair
like the endless times
we have laughed at the ridiculous

Sweet Mystery of Life
Bet Bullock

I don't really know what love is –
the darn thing has so many guises.
Lust, the deceiver, counts for a lot
but so does the feeling of need.
Trouble is…it's full of surprises.

Chemistry plays a big role of course
and struggle for power is frequent.
Possessiveness often raises its head
and sadly, so does obsession. Yet…
that first knowing look is decidedly piquant.

Love songs always add to the illusion
and rose-coloured spectacles are donned.
Hearing becomes very selective…in fact,
senses are totally addled! Love?
Who knows? I'll settle for inordinately fond.

Just Another Day
(After Dylan Thomas's Under Milk Wood)
Win Francis

Morning

The sun was just creeping over St Peter's church spire, turning its silver spike to burnished gold, when the Co-op milk van turned into the cul-de-sac.

"How many today, Mrs Beeley? Is it just the one or are you making a rice pudding for Mr B.'s tea?"

"I'm expecting my in-laws today, so you'd better make it two," she replied.

The clinking bottles changed hands, and with a cheery "Tara," Tom the milkman continued on his round.

Next door the alarm clock rang stridently and Mary Hackett sleepily reached out from under the duvet to switch it off.

"Come on Jim, its half past, you'd better get a move on," she said, and hurried downstairs to put the kettle on.

Jim hauled himself wearily from the comfort of his bed.

"Another day – another dollar," he muttered grumpily as he made his way to the bathroom.

The door of number forty-one opened and Mike Green smelt the early morning air. "It looks as if it's going to be a nice day – I think I'll get the bike out. The exercise will do me good."

His wife Shirley joined him on the doorstep, pulling her faded red dressing gown round her ample frame. "You'd better check the tyres – it's ages since you last used it," she warned.

As Mike disappeared into the shed in the back garden Gavin the paper boy came up the street with his scruffy dog bounding at his heels. "Here, Mongy – take this Mirror to number thirty-seven and don't drop it." The dog took the newspaper in his wide smiling jaws and trotted up to the house.

Just at that moment, the door was flung open and old Mrs.

Barker glared sourly out at Gavin and Mongy. "Will you stop letting your moth-eaten mongrel chew my paper to shreds!" she grumbled.

"He doesn't chew it – he only carries it. He likes to help."

"Well, you're paid to deliver the papers, not your wretched dog!" And with that she slammed the door. A car engine coughed into life as its owner from number twenty-nine eased it off his drive and drove slowly down the cul-de-sac, waving to his wife, who was peering through the net curtains.

"I hope she'll be OK on her own," he thought to himself. She had only been out of hospital a week after a major operation, but he really couldn't afford to have any more time off work. Things were looking pretty dodgy at the firm and they wouldn't need much of an excuse to get rid of one of the workforce.

Eileen the postwoman dropped her trolley at the corner and zig-zagged up the cul-de-sac delivering the morning mail. Several birthday cards for young Sophie – couldn't miss her house with the balloons round the window. A final demand from British Telecom for number twenty-one – this occupant had been out of work ever since his firm had closed. Lack of orders they said – cheap imports from the far East undercutting our prices. More junk mail for number forty-one, offering cheaper car insurance. They'd never owned a car so that would end up in the blue bin for recycling. The latest Saga holiday brochure for the merry widow at number twenty-three – good luck to her, Eileen thought. An air mail letter for the Robertsons – probably from their son in Australia giving them news of the latest addition to the family.

The sun was rising higher in the sky as school children emerged from their houses, hair newly brushed or gelled and coats hanging sloppily from shoulders. Mothers came out holding toddlers by the hand as they skipped to morning nursery full of eager anticipation at what the day would hold.

Old Sam Crawshaw limped down the road leaning heavily on his stick, off to the newsagent for his daily ration of cigarettes.

As he reached the door a young man was pushing his way hurriedly through, almost knocking Sam off his feet.

"Nah then young feller, watch what you're doing!" he admonished.

"Some of us have got work to go to," the youth replied.

"When I was your age I'd done a couple of hours down t'pit by this time in a morning."

"Aye, granddad, and much bloody good it did yer," was the rejoinder, as the young chap ran for his bus.

Tut-tutting to himself, "Kids today!" Sam continued into the paper shop.

The number fifty-three bus pulled out of the terminus to join the queue of traffic at Meadowhead.

The start of just another day on Lowedges.

Evening

Josie Bishop ran up her front path, fishing for her keys as she went.

"Gosh, he'll be home in half an hour – I'll have to get my skates on! It's band practice tonight, so he'll want his tea ready as soon as he gets in."

Tony, her husband, played cornet in a local brass band and he hated to be late for practice. He enjoyed the camaraderie of the band, as well as the couple of pints in the local afterwards.

Josie dropped her bag of shopping on the kitchen floor, pulling off her coat as she did so.

"I ought to have left Mum's a bit earlier," she thought. "She gets so lonely since Dad died – I hate leaving her. Maybe I should ask Tony about her coming to stay with us – but not tonight – it wouldn't be a good time." The sky was changing from hazy blue to pink as the sun dropped lower over Totley Moss, and the moors were silhouetted against the golden glow. A flock of starlings wheeled and tumbled in the evening air above the Parkway before going to roost in the trees beyond.

Jim the paper boy was dashing round with the Sheffield Star.

Mrs Ibbotson, her wispy grey hair screwed up as always in a nest of curlers, saw him coming up her path and flung open her front door. "You're late again! Where have you been 'til this time? I won't get a chance to look at the Star now before t'mister gets home."

"I was kept in for being late back to school after dinner," muttered Tim.

"You'll be late for your own funeral lad," was her parting shot as she shut the door, hastily donning her glasses to have a quiet glance at the Births and Deaths.

A car pulled into the cul-de-sac and up onto the grass verge. Old Bill Eckersley climbed wearily out and stretched his shoulders after a long day at the factory.

"Roll on retirement day," he called to his daughter as he hung his cap in the hall.

"Hello Dad," said Barbara. "Come and sit down– your tea's nearly ready."

A tantalising smell of frying onions wafted in from the kitchen. "That smells good – what're we having?" asked Bill.

"Steak and onions and a jacket potato. I thought I'd treat us as it's your last week at that hell-hole. You've just time to wash your hands and catch the news headlines before I dish up."

Outside, the road was rapidly filling with assorted vehicles, the cars of their owners, the vans and lorries of their firms – all clogging the congested street. Even the grass verges were used as they had never been intended.

The street lamps came on, shedding their weak unnatural light in competition with the setting sun – no contest.

Youngsters reluctantly abandoned their games of football as they were called in for their tea. Some curtains were drawn, some left parted to invite neighbours admiring glances at the new TV set.

The sun finally dipped below the horizon like an extinguished candle. The sky darkened. Evening settled on Lowedges.

The Stand-in
Barbara Thackeray

Sir Edmund Hillary climbed Everest
he's only human, so why can't I?
got a bee in my bonnet now
set off strapped to a guide
haversack on my back
wearing climbing boots, warm clothing, but nothing clumsy
it's a long hard slog
daren't look down or my stomach will churn
hope the guide doesn't fall and take me with him
on second thoughts it's more likely to be the other way round
reached the summit exhausted
my guide congratulated me
I looked up and thought
it can't be much further to heaven

The circus was in town
I came on at short notice
the ringmaster was sick
the show must go on
I was voted to take his place on a majority
smart hat, tailored jacket
but it was the baton which gave me the feeling of authority
as soon as I picked it up I was in command
the cast soon got the idea
maybe they realised there were many ways to use a baton

The panto was in its final week
the lead dancer had sprained an ankle
I came from the chorus line to take over
but I'd always been a follower, not a leader
glitzy outfit, what there was of it
determined to succeed
kicked my legs up as far as my head
and then I did the splits

The Grand Prix
Jean Allen

There was Coulthard and Schumacher, Button and Co.
as I donned the white suit and got ready to go.
The engines were revving, mechanics now still.
I climbed in the Ferrari, heart pounding, until
to my mind came the words of the boss. They were few:
"The eyes of the nation will be watching you."
I knew it was true.

They'd called from the pit lane just moments before,
"Can anyone help us?" The crowd gave a roar,
"Barichello's gone down with the flu, he can't race."
I leapt over the barrier, "Let me take his place,
I can do it," I said without hesitation
and never before had I felt such elation.
ITV? BBC? Harry Gration?

For sixty-nine laps we screamed round the track
faces flattened by G force, front pushed into back.
As the car reached two hundred, it leapt and it danced,
with spectators like meerkats, eyes bulging, entranced.
Cars swerved off the track, they rolled and they spun.
Silver wheels flashed their lightening bolts back to the sun.
Wow, was I having fun!

Every bend and chicane was a challenge, a test
to prove that a girl can compete with the best.
I won by a car length from Schumacher, who
stormed off in a rage, said he'd want a review
of the rules and declared, "Someone must be insane."
But the crowd just went wild and shouted my name
as I splashed my champagne.
The Queen heard all about it and made me a Dame.

The Odd Couple
Win Francis

I was no novice – he was no expert
I was no teacher – he was a slow learner
I was not patient – he was in no hurry
I was not adept – he was so clumsy
I was determined – he was unsure
I guided his hand – his palm was sweaty
I'll teach him the fox trot if it kills me!

Archway
Minnie Douglas

Just to walk in the countryside
breathe in the fresh air
wander through the fields forever –
I don't think I can dare
to dream of castles, or maybe a mansion.
Not knowing what to do,
I think I'll cancel my holiday
to walk through an archway with you.

Grandfather
Barbara Thackeray

I guess we've all heard the song, 'My grandfather's clock was too big for the shelf.' Grandfathers are very fondly thought of by little girls, and I was no exception. Mine lived next door but one to my family: mum, dad, three brothers and myself.

He was my mum's father. Mum liked him living nearby so she could keep an eye on him. He was eighty years old, with a lot of independence. He liked to do a little cooking himself, but mum would always take him anything special she had made.

He kept his little house quite tidy, always washed up himself. Mum would have a good clean every now and again. Hardly anyone had carpet on the floors in those days; linoleum was the norm, with a rug thrown here and there.

Women made the rugs themselves using a type of woven hessian material. They would cut old coats and similar things into small pieces, about one inch by three; they called them clippings. They used a little tool which they called a peg to push one end of a clipping through a hole in the hessian and the other end through the next hole. There was a printed diagram showing where to use different colours to form a pattern. When it was turned over, you had a nice fluffy rug. Mum had made granddad one, which was placed in front of his hearth. It was often taken outside for a good shake.

Grandad had a coal fire as most people did. All his life he had worked down the pit and was allowed a certain amount of free coal, which continued after his retirement.

There were various brass fire irons in the hearth. They were never used for the fire, just ornamental. A brass fender, as we called it, surrounded the hearth. They all needed a weekly clean from mum with the Brasso to keep their high shine. The oven was part of the fireplace and the fire was used to heat it.

Grandad's house was cosy. He had a favourite chair, a wooden rocker, placed near the fire. There was a cushion to sit on and another to rest his back against. There he spent most of his evenings, reading his newspaper and various books that had been passed on to him. There was a smell of tobacco in the place, due to the fact that Granddad loved his pipe. I always thought it had a more acceptable smell than that of a cigarette. He would sit back in his chair and puff on his pipe, then give a sigh of satisfaction.

Grandfather had a kindly face. He hadn't lost much of his hair, only the colour of it. His little moustache was also grey. He had a gold ring on the middle finger of his right hand. When I asked him about it, his eyes looked deep in thought, as if he was thinking back to the past. He told me how he had met my grandma, who was long deceased. They had been courting for a couple of years, when he bought her an engagement ring., and she had then given him the signet ring. It was engraved, 'Frances to Edward.'

There were various things in a cabinet belonging to grandma, which granddad obviously treasured, mostly jewellery, brooches and a bracelet, and best of all, a lovely string of pearls with earrings to match. Grandad said she only wore these on special occasions.

Grandad's clock was indeed too big for the shelf: it was huge. Unlike the clock in the song, which '… was bought on the morn of the day that he was born,' it had been a wedding present from Grandma's family. It was all of six feet tall, and it stood in a corner of the room. He treasured it so much, winding it up once a week to keep it ticking and chiming. It kept perfect time. A large picture of grandma was hanging on the side of it. Sadly, I never knew her, but when I looked at it, I felt love for her. She was dressed appropriately for that period in time. Her hair was taken back off her face, possibly in a bun at the back of her head. A sweet smile was on her face; it would do the Mona Lisa proud. She and Grandfather seemed to be very well matched.

Mum went to his house one evening to check on him. When

she come back, she looked sad. Grandad had fallen into a deep sleep, was how she explained it, in his favourite chair, never to return. He had a little smile on his face of obvious contentment. That was how we must remember him, she said.

The last lines of the song came to mind: 'But it stopped short, never to go again, when the old man died.' It would surely be true, when he was no longer there to give it the weekly wind-up.

The Wishing Well
Sue Roberts

Grey brick covers my frame.
Emptiness lies deep within me
visited most days,
never alone for long.

Birds rest on my shoulders
peer into the pit of my stomach.
People offer a token
then stand in silent anticipation
before they walk away.

The sun warms my outer skin,
fragments of me scatter in the wind.
Rain refills me
as the seasons come and go.

Secrets, wishes,
thoughts and desires
are kept in my cavity
and never revealed.

Hysterectomy
Sue Roberts

Bags packed, I'm on my way
travelling quietly, nothing to say.
I'm worried, but I'll be strong.
I may feel weak, but not for long.

The day comes when they take me down
dressed in white socks, cap and gown.
Efficiently put to sleep at last
to wake up after an hour has passed.

The third day I'm up and walking.
I find a pay phone and can't stop talking.
The fourth and fifth days are very mundane,
the sixth and seventh are much the same.

On the eighth day I'm so upset –
an infection's developed and I'm not home yet.
The ninth day at last is here:
I'm going home! I'm in the clear.

Lanzarote

Jean Allen

As the plane began its ragged descent, Lady Penelope Winthrop cursed the day she had made the decision to take a commercial flight home instead of her usual private charter. She curled up in the crash position. The feel of the leather camera cases under the seat brought little comfort to her. She loved her work, the adventure and excitement. It seemed days, not hours, since she had watched the colourful waterfront of Manaus drop away. She had sighed with satisfaction. Her pictures should make a good bit of money and maybe even bring some needed recognition.

They had been in the air four hours when the storm hit. A lightning strike had made the old DC10 buck like a raging bronco and shortly afterwards had come the chilling announcement, first in Portuguese and then English: "Ladies and gentlemen, we have lost one of our engines and sustained some damage to the hydraulics. We need to make an emergency landing. Please prepare yourselves."

Her last terrified glance out of the window had shown only forest below. They would not stand a chance in that, even if they survived the crash. Minutes later: "Brace yourselves," came the strangled shout over the intercom. She had never felt such fear. A scraping, tearing sound indicated they were flying through trees, then a thud and the whole plane juddered, screeched, hit the ground and swung round 360° as the pilot tried to bring it under control. A quick glance out of the window as they circled giddily showed first a sandy beach, then forest, beach then forest, beach, forest. One final thunderous bang and the plane came to a sudden halt, the cockpit flattened against a large mango tree. There was silence for a few minutes, then people began to struggle out of their twisted seats and extricate themselves from blankets and baggage that were strewn all over. Some moaned in pain, some were bleeding. Penelope found herself able to move and felt for the cameras as she looked for an exit. Minutes later, broken windows let in the sound of excited voices. Faces peered in and the rescue began.

It was 4 pm. Lady Penelope sat uncomfortably on the rough wooden floor of a thatch-roofed shack. Three fellow passengers were with her, two teenagers who had little to say, and one Archibald Newman, who said he was a plumber. It was true he had once been a plumber but the past few years had seen him branch out into more lucrative ways of earning a living. He was now on a police wanted list for several armed robberies. His business associates had suggested he would be better out of the country for a few years and had given him details of a small island called Mocajuba on an Amazon tributary, which they had used before when necessary and where he would be safe.

Several brown skinned children sat silently watching their visitors from the shadows. The smell of cooking came through the open door. A dark skinned man, wearing only tattered shorts, was trying to communicate with them. Penelope's smattering of Spanish enabled her to get the gist of what he was saying. The pilot was dead, also two passengers. The plane was a total wreck. They had landed on a small island with no medical facility. Some people were injured. The weekly commercial boat would arrive in the morning and leave at night for the twenty-four-hour journey to Belem, the Capital City where they could get help. He would ask the boat's owner to take them all on board.

Food was brought in. This was served in relays, there being not enough enamel plates and tin spoons for everyone to eat at once. The meal was a kind of stew, bulked up with what looked like very dry, crumbled cheese. It tasted like sawdust and was in fact the staple diet of these river dwellers, roasted manioc. She had asked what the stew was, and been told it was alligator meat. Archibald Newman didn't know that but had complained anyway and asked for an alternative. He was given the family's three precious eggs, scrambled with a large helping of manioc.

Archibald decided to make friends with Lady Penelope. She knew Spanish and he didn't and he had more reason than most to find out exactly where they were.

Somehow their hosts managed to find enough hammocks for everyone. Penelope began to feel her bruises as she tossed sleeplessly through the cold early morning hours.

One thing was certain, she thought as she struggled stiffly to her feet to receive a tiny cup of sweet black coffee in the morning, there was no washing machine here to get her clothes cleaned up. What a sight she must look. They had salvaged what they could of their baggage. Her radio still worked but could only pick up local Brazilian stations. The Portuguese was too fast to understand. Her hosts listened and said there had been no mention of the missing plane. News traveled slowly in this region, but once the boat reached Belem, the world would know. She wondered how she could repay these kind people who had been so willing to share the little they had with strangers. Breakfast had been pancakes made of roasted manioc spread with some rather rancid margarine and swilled down with more steaming black coffee in which a dab of margarine had been dropped to make it special. She had eaten hungrily.

The boat had docked at dawn and disgorged its sleepy passengers. The rascally captain, dressed in shorts, faded pink shirt and with cheap flip-flops on his feet was quick to take advantage of the situation. Rarely did foreigners come to these isolated islands and now he had a boat load of ostensibly rich passengers. His boat would be photographed, his name emblazoned on the front pages of "O Globo" and maybe in foreign papers too. He made the case clear. Of course he would transport the plane crash victims, even though it meant some of his regular customers might be inconvenienced. His boat was licensed to carry one hundred passengers but regularly carried twice that amount. He would have to comply with regulations and would therefore lose revenue but he was sure he would be recompensed, he said with a glint in his eye and a half-smile on his lips.

Archibald stood and stared at the name on a small canoe tied up at the jetty where the commercial boat was docked. "Our Lady of Mocajuba" it read. Was he actually on Mocajuba? He rushed to find Penelope who was examining her cameras. She had decided that she would leave the potato masher and the set of knives her friend in Belem had asked for as a small gift for the family they had stayed with, but maybe a better reward would be to write an article about the adventure, complete with photographs if the camera still worked. She would sell it to National Geographic or Life magazine. Their faces would be on the front page; Mocajuba would be on the map. She would make sure they got several copies. Her friend in Belem would see to that.

"Hey Pen, managed to find out what this tropical paradise is called?" Archibald interrupted her thoughts, trying not to sound too excited.

"It's something like Mock a jooba," she replied. Archibald strolled out whistling. This place could be O.K. for awhile, until he found something better. He grinned and started to wander round looking for vacant shacks. Somebody was looking out for him.

That afternoon he went down to the dock to see his fellow passengers off. He had made an excuse about suddenly not feeling well enough to travel – due to last night's meal probably, so he would get next week's boat. Penelope stood on the deck as the clumsy wooden craft pulled away, churning the water as it turned into the wide river. The island's small population was out in force to wish them well. She used up her last remaining bit of film, which took in the smiling faces and waving hands. She grimaced as she noticed Archibald had somehow got himself in the front row. Irritating little man, she thought.

Back in Britain, Penelope sent off her pictures. Some weeks later she was gratified to receive a copy of the magazine. She had made the cover. It showed blue sky, palm trees and smiling brown faces, except for one pale face, which she couldn't help noticing but hoped nobody else would as it did rather spoil the effect.

A couple of days later a policeman knocked on her door. He was holding a copy of the magazine.

"I'd like to ask you a few questions about the plane crash," he said.

Next day Penelope once again made the front page. This time a blown up picture of Archibald Newman took centre space in the Daily Telegraph. WANTED MAN IN PLANE CRASH – HIDING OUT IN THE JUNGLE, blazed the headline.

She decided to treat herself to a few weeks in Lanzarote, where she could enjoy her fame and better bank balance before setting out on another assignment. As for Archie, he's probably still in Brazil, as no extradition treaty with the U.K. exists. He may even get to like alligator meat if he stays long enough but I suspect he's probably worked his way down to Rio by now and is lounging on the Copacabana beaches with the beautiful people.

Myths: Ancient And Modern
Bet Bullock

TIME: The Present
PLACE: Somewhere in Space
SET: A Room in a large Palace
CHARACTERS:
ZEUS: Overlord of the Olympian gods and goddesses.
HERMES: Messenger god. Son of Zeus and Hera.
POSEIDON: God of the sea Brother of Zeus.
DEMETER: Goddess of the harvest. Mother of Persephone, daughter of Zeus.
HERA: Goddess of marriage and childbirth. Wife of Zeus.
1st ANGEL: Servant of new god.
2nd ANGEL: Servant of new god.

CHARACTERS REFERRED TO:
SELENA: Goddess of the Moon
ARIES: God of war
CYBELE: Goddess of the Earth.
ATLAS: A Titan who bears the Earth. God of the Sun.
HELIOS: God of the Sun.
PERSEPHONE: Goddess of the underworld. Daughter of Demeter and Zeus.
HEBE: Goddess of youth. Daughter of Zeus and Hera.
HERACLES: Hero of amazing strength. Won immortality for heroic deeds.
HESTIA: Goddess of hearth and home. Sister of Zeus and Hera.
CASTOR: Twin son of Leda and Tyndareus, King of Sparta.

SCENE ONE

ZEUS IS DISCOVERED ON

The stage is lit except for one dark corner.
ZEUS is lying dozing on a sofa but wakes with a start.
A spotlight hits the dark corner and HERMES is standing there.

ZEUS: Who's there?

HERMES advances. The wings on his feet squeak noisily, and the spotlight goes out.
  Oh it's you, Son. I might have known. I was trying to get 40 winks.

ZEUS grimaces as he swings his legs off the sofa, sits up and yawns.
  Do you know how long it is since I slept more than fifteen minutes at a stretch?
HERMES paces about, his face screwed up with the effort of thinking.

HERMES: Er, er, about 2000 years?
ZEUS: And then some, Lad, and then some.
  Don't suppose for one minute you're bringing me good news.
HERMES: I'm afraid not, Father. Good news is hard to come by these days.
ZEUS: Well, out with it then…..and get some oil on those wings of yours before you come here again.
HERMES: I've tried that. Any chance of a new pair?
ZEUS: No way. Do you think I'm made of money?
  The news, lad! The news.
HERMES: Oh yes, right, sorry.
  It's another tragedy I'm afraid. In the Northern Hemisphere this time.

ZEUS: That's a big place. Could you be more specific?

HERMES looks in his notebook.

HERMES: North West England. Longitude 4° Latitude 54°. Shall I put them in the Earthscope?
ZEUS: Yes please.

HERMES walks to a large computer and presses keys. ZEUS rises, walks towards him and sits down in a large swivel chair. The screen crackles and flashes, then becomes clear.

Ah, Morecombe Bay. Are those large fish or mortals in the sea?
HERMES: Mortals I'm afraid. They're cockle pickers and in serious trouble.
ZEUS: So I see, Son, so I see.

ZEUS presses a key on the keyboard.

VOICE: Yes, Sir?
ZEUS: Get Poseidon here at once.
VOICE: Certainly, Sir.

The corner spotlight shows POSEIDON standing there. He joins ZEUS and HERMES at the computer. The spotlight goes out.

POSEIDON: I know what you're going to say, Brother, but it's not my fault.
ZEUS: Do you give me your word that you've not been playing games again?
POSEIDON: I do. That area has always been treacherous and the Spring tide makes it even more so. Mortals have put signs up to that effect.
ZEUS: Well, they've obviously been ignored. Do you know why?

POSEIDON: No, but I'm working on it.
ZEUS: Good. Let me have a report as soon as possible. In the meantime is there anything you can do to help them?
POSEIDON: Nothing. The Moon controls the tides. You could have a word with Selene, but from what I hear, she's fast losing interest in her duties. She's pretty old you know.
ZEUS: (Snapping) We're all pretty old. I wish I'd only one duty to perform. Pretty old indeed!
Get off, get off!

POSEIDON walks to the dark corner. Presses a medallion he wears round his neck, the spotlight comes on, he steps in and the light goes out.

HERMES: Can I go now too, Father? More messages are coming in.
ZEUS: Yes. No, wait. Have we received further reports from Aries on Iraq?
HERMES: Yes, they're being downloaded to you, as are those from Cybele on the latest earthquake.
ZEUS: Ah! Earthquakes. There's not much we can do there. Atlas is getting weary and his tremors are becoming more frequent. Helios is losing his strength too. If the sun fails, or Atlas, it will be the end of the old world and the beginning of the new.
HERMES: What will become of us?
ZEUS: The new world will not be our responsibility. It will have its own gods. I think the reason why we are having less and less influence as the centuries pass is because mortals have already adopted new ones.
HERMES: Should we not try to contact these new Gods?
ZEUS: We've tried many times, and are still trying, but have had no response so far.

The corner spotlight comes on. DEMETER is standing there.

She steps forward and the light goes out

   Now, what is she after?

DEMETER: Hello, Hermes, have you passed the message on yet?
HERMES: Er no, I forgot.
DEMETER: Thought you would.
ZEUS: Can't you see I'm busy? What do you want?
DEMETER: You're always busy these days. Look, I know I'm only one of your many mistresses but your daughter Persephone will be arriving shortly and I really think you should make some time for her.
ZEUS: I'll see what I can do. If that's all, I'd be glad if you'd push off.

The spotlight comes on and HERA is standing there.

ZEUS: Blast! She would have to show up now.

HERA steps forward and the light goes out.

HERA: What's she doing here?
ZEUS: Just going I hope.
DEMETER: I've as much right as you to be here!
HERA: No you haven't! I'm his wife. I'm surprised you've got the nerve, knowing what I insisted on Zeus doing to a lot of his bastard children.
DEMETER: Forcing him to turn them in to animals? I do know and you're disgusting. Well, he can't do that to mine, Hades will see to that. I doubt if you've still got influence over Zeus now anyway.
ZEUS: Stop it you two! I won't have this infernal wrangling every time you meet. Go, Demeter, I'll speak to you later.
DEMETER: Huh! Very well. But don't forget about Persephone.

DEMETER walks in to the corner, presses her medallion, the spotlight comes on, she steps into it and the light goes out.

HERA: Hello Hermes, are you well?
HERMES: Not bad, Mother, thank you.
ZEUS: Well, Wife, what do you want? And make it snappy.
HERA: I'm having a few people in to dinner next week I'd like you to put in an appearance.
ZEUS: Who's coming?
HERA: Your daughter Hebe with her husband Heracles. Our sister Hestia, you haven't seen her for awhile, and Castor and Pollux hope to make their way here.
ZEUS: I'm surprised you've invited Pollux, or have you forgiven me for my one night stand with his mother Leda?
ZEUS: It's not certain he was your son. Anyway, Caster wouldn't come without him and they're such stars. They brighten up any party.
ZEUS: I'd make an odd number....oh, I know! I'll bring Aphrodite.
HERA: Over my dead body! You make such a fool of yourself with her and she's not the slightest bit interested in you.
ZEUS: Rubbish! You're just jealous as usual. Anyway, look, I'd be a spare man, you don't need me.
HERA: I do. Be reasonable. It's not as if I call on you very often.
ZEUS: Oh, all right. I'll bring Selene; come to think of it I've a bone to pick with her about the tides.
HERA: I don't want any arguing. You know how easily Hestia gets upset.
ZEUS: Athene's not coming then?
HERA: You must be joking! I vowed I'd never put you two together again.
ZEUS: Well, daughter or no daughter, I'm not having her lecturing me. Love and Peace! Y'know, I reckon she was responsible for all those flower people. I couldn't prove it but it smacked of her all right.

HERMES: I'm not invited then?

HERA: Certainly not! After the way you behaved last time? Showing off, that's what it was. You get that from your father, not me.

ZEUS: (Smiling) What did you do, lad?

HERMES: Oh, I had too much nectar and gave an exhibition of fancy flying.

HERA: Whirling about like that! He broke that bust of our grandson Pan.

HERMES: I told you I'll get another one done for you.

HERA: Yes, and I'm still waiting.

ZEUS: And now so am I – for you to clear off!

HERA: Very well. I'll get a message to Selene that you'll call for her. I know you and your convenient loss of memory.

She walks to the dark corner, presses her medallion, the spotlight comes on and goes out.

ZEUS: I think I'll recall some of those medallions. It's too easy for folk to drop in unannounced.

The corner spotlight comes on revealing POSEIDON. He advances and the spotlight dies.

POSEIDON: I've discovered the source of the trouble. It's the Underworld.

HERMES: Uncle Hades?

ZEUS: I'm not surprised. Unfortunately, his power to tempt mortals doesn't seem to have diminished.

POSEIDON: I haven't got all the details, but the buzz is, those mortals we saw on the screen had language difficulties and that was taken advantage of by their employers, who certainly knew the risks involved.

HERMES: Why is Hades so wicked?

ZEUS: He abuses his power. I blame myself for giving him the ammunition. I was responsible for Pandora and her box, you see. I misused my power and presented her as a gift to mankind. I forbade her to open the box, but you know what women are.

HERMES: She opened it?

ZEUS: Of course she did, and out came all the evils of the world, such as disease, death, lies, theft, you name it, which spread throughout nature.

HERMES: With your experience of women, you must have known what would happen!

ZEUS: Power can corrupt, Son, even the best of us. At that time, well, I admit I did some rotten things. It's not easy being chief you know. A lot of people tried my patience. Some still do.

POSEIDON: We've all done things we're sorry for, brother. Don't be pious, it doesn't suit you.

HERMES: Ah! Look at the screen. Mortals have sent one of their mechanical birds to help rescue some of them.

ZEUS: Good. Hades will be furious of course. Fortunately he doesn't control the majority of mortals.

POSEIDON: Perhaps their new Gods have something to do with that.

ZEUS: Let us hope so. They're going to need all the help they can get. We must try harder to contact these new Gods! Maybe we're not too old to learn something.

POSEIDON: What could they possibly teach us?

ZEUS: Humility perhaps?

Zeus leans over and switches off the computer.

Look, I'm knackered, so why don't both of you get lost? I'm going back to my sofa and if I'm lucky Hypnos will take pity on me and let me fall into the arms of Morpheus.

CURTAIN FALLS

Two ANGELS walk on to the apron.

FIRST ANGEL: Just finished your shift?
SECOND ANGEL: Yes, thank goodness. Listening to all that chatter from outer space is driving me barmy. You're lucky you've only Earth to deal with.
FIRST ANGEL: And it's enough, I can tell you. Some of the tricks they get up to you wouldn't believe. Will they never learn?
Are you still getting that peculiar signal?
SECOND ANGEL: Yes, and more often lately. They're persistent, I'll give 'em that.
FIRST ANGEL: Are you any nearer to understanding it?
SECOND ANGEL: No. As I said to the supervisor, it's all Greek to me.

FINAL CURTAIN.

Silver Birch
Win Francis

I stand on the brow of a hill and from my top most branches I can see the river in the distance, snaking its way along the valley like a silver ribbon. Fishermen cast their lines into its sparkling depths; cattle graze lazily along its banks and water buttercups add a splash of yellow.

Young lovers lie in my gentle shade, their faces dappled with sunlight. I bend my branches over them to give them more privacy. They wander off hand in hand towards their future, whatever it may hold, like so many I have sheltered over the years. Styles and fashions change, but young love remains the same.

Here comes an elderly couple with their dog, taking their daily walk to keep their old joints mobile. I know how they feel — when the wind howls and the rain lashes, I get the odd ache in my limbs.

A squirrel has made his home in a cleft in my branches, which gives me a lot of pleasure as I watch its antics. A group of small children arrive with their teacher and start to skip round me, singing nursery rhymes, their eyes sparkling and their cheeks glowing with the effort.

Some days, families picnic in my shade, Mum spreading the blanket, children squabbling about who sits next to Dad and who has the Harry Potter mug. Most of them take their litter home, but some are less thoughtful and I am left with paper and cans and other rubbish among my roots.

Sometimes, campers and hikers take my papery bark to kindle their campfires, which is fine so long as they don't go too deep. That can make my sap bleed.

I'm very popular with the birds, especially the blue tits, who hang upside down, picking insects from under my leaves. I keep my leaves well into the autumn, when they turn yellow before finally falling to reveal my graceful silhouette against the winter sky.

Botanists call me Betula Pendula, but you will know me by my popular name, which I prefer: Silver Birch.

Prayer
Win Francis

What do I want from life?
Not an easy ride, but a joyous one.
Let me be happy, but make others happy too.
Let me hear music soaring heavenwards
and see drama unfold around me.
Let me feel the love of others and give my love as willingly.
Let me give comfort where there is heartache
and find a sympathetic shoulder to cry on.
Let me hear birdsong in the morning
and see a golden sunset at dusk.
Let me smell the perfume of honeysuckle
and feel the smoothness of polished wood.
Let me walk the hills and dales of my beloved Derbyshire
and I will be fulfilled.

Good Samaritan
Bet Bullock

MONDAY

Hello love…oh dear, you do look rough. 'Ere, give me them milk bottles. I'll put 'em out for you…I'd stay in and keep warm if I were you…..shopping? Well, I'm poppin' down in a bit, can I get you anything? Oh, you thought somebody might pop in…. made a list…good…course it's no trouble, it'd be a poor world if you couldn't help a neighbour.

TUESDAY

Was that you knockin' on t'wall? Thought it was, I said to Ted that'll be Annie knockin'. How are you today, feelin' better? Oh, not so good. Well, never mind, how about a nice cup o' tea?

Oh! I see you managed a bit o' breakfast; while kettle's boiling I'll wash these few pots. Make your bed? 'Course I will and I'll tell you what, I'll bring you round a nice plate of stew later. I've made plenty, it'll stretch to six instead of five. Must dash off in a minute. I'm taking my youngest t'doctors for an injection…what? Oh, you've nothin' to read. Well I've a magazine you can 'ave …library books? Oh, I don't know…ah, well, if t'woman knows what you like…. look, I've told you it's no trouble.

WEDNESDAY

'Ere's your library book…oh, you've read that one, well other's a thick 'un…

…eh? Which bag? Oh, this carrier…well, I do all my washing on a Monday as a rule. You should 'ave said.

I go to my mum's today and do for 'er. Aye, well, I suppose I could put 'em to soak before I go. Now I must dash…oh, a cup o'tea…..well, it'll have to be a quick 'un…see you haven't washed up....now, now, I was only jokin'…no, I've telled you it's no trouble.

THURSDAY

I've hung your washin' out, seein' as it's a nice day…Why aren't you dressed? You should 'ave said you wanted your vest. I'll fetch it in, it's just about dry. You won't catch your death! Oh, all right, don't upset yourself, I'll nip home and see if I can find you one. Eee, come to think, I've got a new 'un I bought for my mum's birthday. I'll get her another. …Nay, I haven't asked you for t'money have I? I know you've only got your pension…oh, it's due today is it? Will they let me get it? Oh, I see, you've sorted it…I think it'll have to be this afters, though, I've a lot on this mornin'…look, do you want your vest or your pension first? I've only one pair of 'ands….oh, for goodness sake, stop cryin'! I'm not cross with you…you're not a nuisance. Look, I'll make you a nice cup o' tea before I go.

FRIDAY
I know I'm a bit late poppin' in but I've 'ad all my house to clean, got a bit behind this week what with one thing and another…now then, I didn't say it were runnin' after you that did it…look, I'm doing bacon and egg for tea for my lot. I'll bring you a bacon sandwich round…oh, you've had sommat to eat, managed it yourself thinkin' I weren't comin'! Well, that's good, feelin' better are you?…I don't suppose you are 100%. Who is these days? Look, I've time to make you a cup o'tea while I wash these pots and tidy up a bit….o'course it's no trouble.

SATURDAY
Just seen yer light come on, I've been worried sick. Where the hell 'ave you been all day? What? Who's broken your winda? Well, who do you think? It were our Ted 'ere. I were that upset when you didn't come t'door – wan't I, Ted? – knocking and knocking I were, thought you were lying unconscious or sommat…look, stop goin' on about your bloody winda, nobody in't street had seen hide nor hair of ya…forgotten about it? Forgotten what?…booked it weeks since? What y're on about?…coach trip? You've been to seaside?…..well, can you catch your breath! Did you hear that Ted? She's been out enjoying her bloody sen...aye, you're right, let's geroff home. It's certainly true what they say. There's one born every minute.

Jason Paul
Sheila Kelshaw

What is the matter with Jason Paul?
He cannot walk but he can crawl.
He's into the kitchen, he's into the hall.
We do love our Jason Paul.

He has two teeth and two fat cheeks,
the cutest little nose, and when he falls asleep
he curls his tiny toes. And now he's one,
his crawling done, he walks with heart of ease.
He kicks a ball and rolypoles
in front of our settee.

And now he's three, he talks to me
with words I understand,
such words as: tea, toast, and football!
and dirty face and hands!

Goody Two-Shoes
Heather Norton

You're no goody-goody.
I'm a goody two-shoes.
You've got two left feet.
I'm well heeled.
You're poor like a church mouse.
I'm being catty.
You would go all the way.
I'd say, "No way, Jose!
Go find yourself a Spanish senorita."

A Character
Minnie Douglas

Well I suppose my partner was just that. When my children, all seven, were told to get out by my drunkard husband, who else would have taken us in, even if he was a friend of my husband?

So the second half of my life began. He was nine years younger than I. He had a heart as big as a frying pan. He wasn't good looking. He dressed very flashy and wore a tee shirt much too small for work. Everyone loved him. Nothing was too much trouble. He would help anyone and give his last penny to my children. They all grew up to love this big, loving man.

Christmas was his favourite time. He could dress as Father Christmas for the party for the children held in the local pub. He was like a clown, always wanting to make people laugh. The old people also demanded him at Christmas parties and he would always oblige, wearing my big sheepskin. He even dressed as a woman and won first prize for his Easter bonnet, going to a few pubs and saying, "I've worn these tights all day, love, and never laddered them!"

Wherever we went on holiday, people wanted to follow. He could tell jokes about anything and everybody, never offending anyone.

He was a lorry driver and delivered cars, coming home in a different car each night, always saying he would not have a Mini because he had a Minnie at home.

My children grew up and left home. Each time Roy came home, the first thing he would say was,"Has Faith rung? Has Heather rung and Robert?" And so on, through all my children's names. Sometimes, when I received a letter from my eldest in Australia, I did not show it until after he had eaten his tea, and you would always guess he would have a little cry. He just liked all the children around him. He was like a child himself.

Unrequited Love
Bet Bullock

Stephen is sixty-eight years of age. Six months ago he fell down the stairs and fractured his spine. This resulted in him being completely paralysed and he is confined to a wheel chair in a nursing home.

'You've got a letter, Stephen,' said Matron, waiving an envelope at me. 'Shall I open it for you?'

Stupid sod! Of course I want her to open it. Am I supposed to use my bloody teeth? I give her a hard stare and say, 'Yes please.'

She rips open the envelope. 'It's a Christmas card.' She bends the card so it will stay open, places it on my bookstand and walks away. I'm not her favourite patient.

'Who's this from then?' I muttered as I reached for the card.

'Heard on the grape vine you'd had an accident but no details other than you'd fallen down and were in a home. If you've damaged yourself, I presume you were sober at the time. Best wishes, your old, in more ways than one, girl friend, Sally. X'

Sally. My little Sally Cartwright. Well blow me down! Suppose it's too much to hope that she might visit me? Course it is. Wouldn't want her to see me like this anyway. She still cares about me though, that's something. Yep, that's definitely something.

Oh Sally, Sally. It's a bloody tragedy things didn't work out for us. They should have done. From first meeting we clicked. How old would we be then? Let me think. I reckon I'd be twenty, so she'd be seventeen. Young and daft we were. Didn't half have some fun though, eh? Larking about in that big old house in the country the firm evacuated us to – dashing off every lunch time into that long grass. We didn't actually make love – well, you didn't in them days, did you? Oh boy, we came damn close to it though, we sure did. God! I was crackers about that lass, even though she bit her nails and could never button her coat up right. She went for me too, then, I know she did. Bloody war! Right age at the wrong time, that was us. But for that, we might have….oh, don't go down that road again, you fool! Anyway, can't blame the war: we came through it. Lots didn't.

Funny, really. We didn't communicate much. I was all over the place, so was she. I remember one letter. It finally reached me in Italy. She obviously hadn't met anybody and I hadn't. I bought her a brooch in Venice. Told her not to lose it 'cos it had cost me twenty thousand lira. Didn't tell her that was about three quid. Wonder if she's still got it? I sent her a photo of me and old whatsisname – Reg, or was it Ron? – in a gondola we were. She was right taken with that. There was an understanding. I reckon we both knew that.

And then I flaming blew it, didn't I. We were de-mobbed, wedding was two weeks off and I had to go and get pissed as a newt. Made a right bloody fool of meself. Picked a fight with a bloke and when she got me out of the pub and took me to her sister's I chucked up all over her new stair carpet. Her brother-in-law never liked me. Thought I weren't good enough for her. Told me to get out and come back when I was sober. I did, but it were too late. I reckon they worked on her. She said they didn't, it was her decision not to marry me. I didn't believe her though. I think it might still have worked out if my ma hadn't gone to see her. I know me ma was upset but she could be a bit of a fishwife when she got riled up. Anyway, that were that.

I should never have jumped into marrying Mavis. Christ! If Sally's family didn't think I was good enough for her, what would they have said about me and Mavis? Now, she were real gentry, she were that. Big house, pots of money – she was older than me, o'course. I never really loved her though. Not like I did Sally. That's why I went back to see Sally again. To see if I'd got over her. I hadn't. The minute I saw her I knew I hadn't. She looked a bit dropped on when I met her outside where she worked. After a bit, though, she seemed pleased to see me, or I would never have told her I still loved her, that I'd made a mistake getting married and if she'd reconsider I'd get a divorce. The look on her face told me it were no go. That really hurt, did that. Can't say I blamed her though. Married six weeks and there I was crawling back to her. If she thought I was a wimp before, I sure proved it. So I went back to Mavis.

We made a go of it. Had two boys. Can't say I was a good father apart from doling out money to 'em. Didn't have much in common, me not being a sporty type. Mavis weren't either, she were a mumsy mum, took good care of 'em and me. Wasn't home all that much. Job had a big social side but Mavis didn't go for that. Now, Sally would have loved it, she liked a drink and meeting folk. She was a big United fan, could talk football with the best of 'em. I never really got her out of my mind. Tried to, but she kept coming back.

Mavis didn't go a bundle on sex. I overheard her once saying to her friend, 'Steve's not the demanding type, thank goodness. Twice a month is plenty for me.' I shouldn't have done it I suppose, but when I heard that I thought, right. I waited 'til that month were nearly out and then did it twice in the last week. Then, in the first week of the next month, I did it twice again. She got her own back, o'course. Moved in to her own bedroom and locked the door every night. Not that I went short. I'd allus had a few on the side. Well, it's a man's nature, innit? We're made different.

Then I met Sally again. Mavis died sudden and after the funeral I took the boys – well, I say boys, they were in their late teens by then. Anyway, I took 'em up to Sheffield for a few days and, as I were there, I took a chance that Sally hadn't married and looked her up in the phone book. I struck lucky, so called on her. She were dumbfounded to see me but I persuaded her to come to the pub. I told her I was a widower with two boys and I'd got a chance of running a pub down where I lived. It were no lie, I had, and I thought that might interest her. It were no go again, though. She'd got a good job and was being promoted. She'd no desire to get married to anybody. I suppose I should be grateful she didn't say, '...particularly you.' We chatted for a bit about our lives and parted friends.

'Do you want a drink of tea love?'

Christ! She made me jump. At least I think I jumped, you can't tell. I think Gladys is a bit deaf; she stuck her face about two inches from mine.

'Yes,' I said. She poured out the tea, stuck a straw in it and put it where I could reach it. I sucked a bit then said, 'Thank you, Gladys, but don't come as near to me as that again or I won't be able to trust meself.' She giggled.

Now, where were I? Oh yeah. Back to wandering down memory lane. It's all I do these days, apart from reading and sleeping. Can't watch television, it's such a load of tripe.

I didn't take the pub. They insisted on having a landlady and I weren't going to marry any old body. Once bitten, twice shy. I did remarry eventually, though. Well, I couldn't look after the lads, could I, and they seemed in no hurry to leave me. Rose, you called her.

Well, she were rosy all right, I couldn't keep up with her. Proper little sex bomb she were and she liked a drink. She weren't too happy when she found she were pregnant. That's what getting pissed together does for you, wits straight out the window. We had a girl and she were a beauty. I knew she'd break a few hearts when she grew up. Rose and me had our ups and downs. When she were mad at me she used to say, 'I don't know what you want. I look good, I cook good and I'm a dab hand at the other thing.' She were sparky, were Rose. It were my fault we broke up. I enjoyed going to the pub with the lads. She went with me before little Sandra were born, but then stopped. I didn't see why I had to an'all. Anyway, she gave me the big heave ho and kept the kid. I was in touch for awhile but she married another bloke and moved away. My two lads had both gone into the army soon after I remarried, so I needn't have bothered. I lost touch with them an'all. After a while on me own, I decided to look Sally up again. I reckoned she'd be retired by now and might want a bit of company.

I caught a train and rang her up from the station. She said it wasn't very convenient but I told her I was only in town for the day. We met at the pub opposite the station. Well, I thought, if I'm out of luck again, no point in travelling miles for nothing. I bought us a couple of drinks. By gum, she'd clapped weight on and I said so. She was still the same old Sally though and we had a good laugh. But that's all we had. She said she was expecting company and couldn't stay long. I asked her why she bothered to come and she said she was intrigued by the way I kept getting in touch with her. She thought I'd have forgotten her years ago. I told her I was fancy-free again and this was her last chance. She fell about and said, 'My God, you're worse than a sticking plaster!' I know it sounds daft but just for a moment it was if all the years disappeared and we were back as we were. Laughing and taking the mickey. I asked her if she'd ever loved me and she said, 'Of course I did, at first, but a lot of water has gone under the bridge since we were kids. I realised I loved your company but there was no way I could marry you.' It didn't hurt as much this time. We parted good friends again.

So, here's where I've finished up. No family, no nothing. It won't be for long, though; the Doc says my liver's shot. Ah, well, look on the bright side: I'm fed and watered by a bevy of maidens and I've still got my memories. And now Sally's sent me a card, so, even though she never loved me like I did her, I reckon I must have been a bit special to her. Yeah, a bit special.

Oh, bugger! Me tea's gone cold. 'Gladys!'

Yasmin
Jean Allen

The Province of Kerala, India

Yasmin sat on the old wooden bench in the shade of a tamarind tree and allowed the warmth of the tropical garden to envelop her in its serenity. Its gentle breezes and birdsongs quietened her spirit. Her thick black hair was pulled back into a band and tied at the nape of her neck. Her plain green sari clung damply to her back. Through the trees, she could see the house a couple of hundred yards away. Large open windows gave glimpses of people bustling to and fro inside. All fourteen bedrooms were being swept and dusted, ready for the guests who would flood in today and tomorrow. Her efficient, stern mother would be presiding over the mountains of food that were being prepared in the large kitchen. Masses of flowers were being placed in every free bit of space and best clothes had already been taken out of storage for the occasion.

Yasmin sighed. She loved this place. Tomorrow would mark the beginning of a change in her life that would eventually take her thousands of miles away to live among strangers. Tomorrow she would become engaged to Sanjit and just one week later they would be married. Convention decrees that the engagement ceremony take place in the bride's home and the wedding in the bridegroom's. Sanjit, however, came from a poorer family and their smaller house would not be able to accommodate everyone, so in this case both ceremonies would take place here.

A thin, stooping figure approached through the trees, carrying a large glass of something cool and refreshing. Joseph sat down on the bench beside his daughter, handing her the glass and patting her on the shoulder as he did so. He loved all his children, the three girls and one boy, but this one was the first child, and somehow special. He looked at her lovely face and as she looked back, he could see tears were gathering in her large brown eyes. He knew they were not tears of regret. She truly loved Sanjit. He had been angry at first, when the young couple announced to him that they wished to marry. This flouting of convention had upset the family. He had expected to arrange a good marriage for his daughter, someone good and kind and wealthy. Sanjit's family were honourable. Good people. Sanjit's grandfather had once worked the land for Joseph's family. He knew that they were not well off. Both families shared one common ambition, and that was to give their children a college education. It was while studying to be social workers that Yasmin and Sanjit fell in love.

Father and daughter sat for a while in silence, then walked slowly back to the house hand in hand. The next day would be a blaze of crowds, ritual, symbolism and feasting. Blessings would be received at the special Mass. One week later it would all be repeated at the wedding, on an even grander scale, and her new life would begin. Yasmin went into her room and caressed the two new saris, loving the rich colours and the silky feel of the material. She fingered the special gold jewellery, which she would be entitled to wear as a married woman in just one week's time, and began to feel excited.

Sheffield, England, Six Months Later

Yasmin hurried down the winding lane, shivering as the first wet snowflakes of winter spattered her face and crept down the neck of her jacket. Her sturdy brown legs were goose pimpled and the thin skirt and open toed shoes offered little protection. It had been a difficult morning in the Nursing Home. Mrs. Chantonville had kicked her in the stomach as she knelt to prize the resisting feet into soft slippers. Old John had looked on mutely from his wheelchair, waving his one good hand, anxious to attract help for her but he was not noticed. She had been left to work alone, given the jobs no-one else wanted. Not all the residents were bad, but some resented her dark skin and made hurtful remarks, which no one refuted. She blinked back the tears. This was no place to cry; she would wait until she got home. She pushed back the damp strands of hair that had escaped from her headband. Soon it would be dusk. Leafless trees waved their skinny branches in her face as if they too mocked this stranger. Sanjit would not come to meet her today as he sometimes did. His work would keep him busy until six o'clock. She felt very alone.

Three months after their marriage, Sanjit had left his work with street children in Kerala Province and come to Sheffield to gain more qualifications, leaving his young wife with her family until he found a place for them to live. He found a flat on Lowedges and Yasmin joined him.

She dug her hands deeper into the shallow pockets of her jacket as the lights of the large housing estate came into view. Minutes later, she was climbing the concrete stairs to the small two-bedroom flat. She unlocked the door quickly, entered and locked it securely behind her. How she hated being alone. She turned the gas fire on high, noticing the thin curtains moving slightly as the wind sneaked through old metal window frames. She made a cup of tea with boiled milk and sugar, then flopped onto the double mattress on the floor, still in her jacket, and cried. She cried for India; for her strong mother and kindly father; for the lost companionship of her fun-loving sisters; for the servants, who were more like friends. She looked round the small room and cried for the spacious family home where she had spent her happy childhood; for the huge grounds filled with a wilderness of sweet smelling plants and trees. She cried for the church, the daily Mass, the ceremony and ritual.

Suddenly she realised Sanjit would soon be home. Everything was better when he was there. He is a good, kind, hard-working man, she thought. I love him and he loves me. Somehow I will survive in this cold country where everyone lives boxed-in lives, where strangers are often looked on with suspicion, and where old people are not respected and children are rude. She rose, washed her tear-stained face and went into the kitchen to prepare the evening meal. She cut up spinach, grated coconut, chopped chicken with the large cleaver she had brought from home, and cooked the rice.

Although shy, the young couple gradually got to know their

neighbours and friendship developed with an older couple over shared meals, table games, watching videos and trips to Meadowhall. There, Yasmin did not feel such an outsider and mingled happily with the throng of shoppers. Sanjit always bought her something, usually clothes. He was generous and wanted his young wife to be happy.

One night, about a year later, Sanjit bounced in with some news. He had the offer of a job: more money, wider experience, and it was in Southall, where he had friends. It would be warmer down there. His friends would help him find a place to live and transport him, with their few belongings, in his car. Then Sanjit would return for Yasmin and they would make the final trip to London together by train.

"You'll be able to go to English classes, and there are better job prospects for both of us," he told her.

It was almost dark when, a month later, they squeezed the last cardboard box into the estate wagon and Sanjit climbed into the small remaining space beside the driver. Yasmin wanted to cling to him, beg him never to leave her on her own again, but she didn't. Tonight she would stay with the old couple in their home and tomorrow she would close up the empty flat and hand in the key. Sanjit would come back and take her to their new home - just a bed-sit this time, but more expensive than the Lowedges flat. The old couple worried about them and hoped it would not be long before they found new friends. They would miss Yasmin and Sanjit, and as they waved goodbye at the station next day, it was obvious the feeling was mutual.

"You will come and visit us, won't you?" asked the young couple.

"Of course we will," they replied, and they did.

"God ... has made of one blood all nations of men to dwell on the face of the earth." Who could give you a blood transfusion? Anyone in the world who matched your blood type, even Osama bin Laden!

Time

Barbara Thackeray

As I open my eyes this morning, the first thing I see on my bedside cabinet is the clock. Its face looks rather evil, but it's only 5:30 am, so maybe that's just a figment of my imagination.

The clock is a dictator, and as such, it tells me when to get up, to get meals ready, to go to bed. In fact, it controls almost everything I do in my everyday living. I need to wind it daily to keep it breathing. It ticks constantly; that is its heartbeat. I guess if it stopped ticking, I would think it was dead.

Not able to sleep any more, I roll out of bed. My bedroom is a prison. I am in solitary confinement. It has low lighting, hardly enough to read by.

I open the curtains to see the stars, lamps in the sky, soon to disappear as the dawn breaks.

The silver balloon of a moon, floating among the dark hairy clouds, mysteriously fades away.

The cat from next door, with the eye of a vulture, is looking for its first victim of the day, possibly a bird which has come to feed from my bird table.

The sky is now a picture postcard, a dream to paint, as the grey and haggard clouds have been replaced by soft blue and fluffy white. The horizon is a picture to behold, with streaks of vibrant colour across the meeting place of earth and sky. The sun, a huge ball of yellow tinted with orange, is just beginning to show itself above it. At this moment, it resembles Humpty Dumpty sitting on the wall. Within a matter of minutes, it looks as if it has been kicked into position as it takes its place in the sky.

A vision of light, and a new day has begun. Our neighbourhood, quiet as a morgue at night, suddenly comes to life, beginning with the early morning workers, such as Jack the postman and Bill the milkman. The remainder of my neighbours follow at intervals, as they make their way to their jobs.

Gradually, the army of cars, parked as neatly as a platoon in the parking area, all march away.

A True Story
Minnie Douglas

My partner, who had died and been cremated, finished up in different parts of my garden. When I first received his ashes, I bought a large tub for the back. I put the ashes in. It was one third full. I filled it up with soil, planted his favourite tree in it, said a prayer, and that was that.

A few days later, I noticed the tree had died, so I emptied the soil out in different parts of the garden. The ashes seemed to have doubled. I then put a geranium and some marigolds in the tub. Not long after this, a friendly neighbour pointed out to me that there seemed to be something like blood oozing out of the bottom of the tub.

"Well," I sad, "that's something Roy is trying to tell me." He hated geraniums and marigolds, so I once again emptied the soil and this time planted a rose tree. It is really beautiful. When people ask me where Roy is buried, my reply is, "His legs are at the top of the garden and his arms at the bottom."

As a bit of a comedian, he'd have laughed his socks off.

A Sporting Dream

Dave Lightfoot

The event was at the Crucible in 1995;
I was playing well when the auditorium came alive.
It was during the third frame
When I really made my name.
I got a 147 against the whirlwind White;
from that day on I'll never forget that night.
That was my only buzz, as he was the eventual winner
but I got recognised as a hero and not a sinner.
I didn't get despondent when I'd lost
as I'd made my money at other people's cost!
To this day I'll always treasure that cue
and I suppose it's what most people would do.

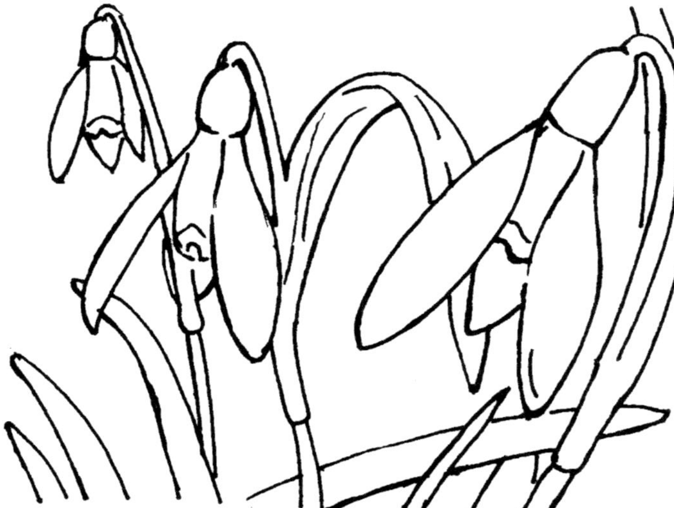

Snowdrops
Jean Allen

She stared out of the window at the unfamiliar garden. The earth was hard. Brown stems of last year's flowers stood like clumps of lonely sentinels, speaking only of what once had been, offering no glimmer of hope that things might change. Would she ever get used to this place where everyone was a stranger? Would the loneliness ever go away? He would have found something to brighten the day, remembered a joke or some silly episode of their early days together. He would have made something of this garden, accepted it as a challenge. She could see nothing in it to lift the dreariness she felt.

A robin hopped along the path, sat for a moment by a rock and flew off but not before she had noticed a little patch of green where he had rested. Was something alive in this dead place? She went out, shivered as the east wind ruffled her hair and picked her way across the broken paving stones .

They were growing by the side of the rock – one small clump of snowdrops, so fragile that even a light touch would have crushed the tiny stem, yet strong enough to push through icy soil, bend to the storms and give hope of better days to come as their white bells opened. She looked around and saw more of them hidden in the debris of last year's plants. Some were large enough to be cut and put in her small crystal vase.

She poured herself a cup of tea and sat at the table to drink it, letting the cup warm her hands. The snowdrops looked on in approval.

"That's better," they seemed to say. "Spring is on the way, and when it comes, everything will look brighter." She smiled at the little white flowers. "Well, if you can make it through the winter I'm sure I can," she said and began to make a list of things to do.

Gallant Galanthus
Jean Allen

Tiny earthly stars
signalling that Spring is coming
new beginnings.
Fragile flowers but strong enough
to break through frosty ground
pushing their way
through last year's fallen leaves,
withered stems.
A cut glass vase filled with pearly smiles
the snowdrops on my kitchen table.

Saints And Sinners
Bet Bullock

Confession is good for the soul
we're told, but is this always true?
Take, let's say, a spy who's a mole –
well, that's the last thing he should do.

And less likely still, people who've erred
and are anxious to confess. To appease
their conscience, their guilt's transferred
by mea culpa with consummate ease.

Where's the good for the soul of a man
who confesses to anything that's said?
After denying for hours he no longer can,
so, exhausted, takes to lying instead.

And what of those who mislead us,
the chosen who promise the earth?
When their promises crumble like pie crust
what will their confessions be worth?

So confess your sins and all will be well?
It's a saying as ancient as time.
Yet many good people, history tells,
chose death, thus remaining sublime.

Old Age
Frank Hooley

Walk steadily, not hurriedly
Talk genially, not fretfully
Eat heartily, not frugally
You still have time

Sleep peacefully, not restlessly
Wake eagerly, not peavishly
Dress stylishly, not slovenly
You still have time

Write pleasantly, not chidingly
Read avidly, not sparingly
Sing lustily, not drearily
You still have time

Love tenderly, not jealously
Loathe fleetingly, not bitterly
Laugh merrily, not scornfully
You still have time

Go graciously, not grudgingly
When it is time

Spice Girls
Frank Hooley

In the culinary art
We can each play our part
If we use all that nature supplies
There's cumin and rue
Garlic, cinnamon too
Employ them to spice up your pies

Add sweet marjoram
To the strawberry jam
Horseradish to tingle the tongue
Season your porridge
With basil and borage
Your breakfast will taste like a song

Take fennel and clove
Warmed up on the stove
Add rosemary into the stew
Toss in a few chives
It will brighten the lives
Of folk who have little to do

Use coriander
If you wish to pander
To those who have exotic fads
Add saffron and sage
You'll be all the rage
With snooty young lasses and lads

Mint, nutmeg, dill, balm
Will do little harm
When chopped up with parsley and thyme
Use plenty of mustard
To flavour your custard
Which neatly doth finish my rhyme

Memories
Jean Allen

London, 1962

The Mother's Hospital in Clapton was run by the Salvation Army. I had enjoyed my first six months of midwifery training there. Now it was time to move out of that sheltered environment and continue my training on district. This turned out to be very different from the secure hospital setting I had become used to.

My first real challenge was learning to ride a bike. Few midwives had cars in those days, so I learned on the roads of east London, leaping off and dragging the bike onto the pavement every time a lorry rumbled past. Eventually, I learned to manage well enough.

The gas and air machine was anchored firmly onto the pannier at the back, the black Gladstone bag slung over the right handlebar. The large metal bedpan, tastefully disguised in black plastic, was clutched in my left hand, with which I also tried to maintain some grip on the handlebar. I still wobbled dangerously when a lorry passed with only inches to spare, but I didn't get off nearly so often. The incentive to stay on was strong because, once off, it took considerable skill and time to get everything back in place, including me.

It was a cold night in Dagenham. Snow clouds which had been hovering all day now began to empty their contents. Sister Morris and I were alone in the house. A baby was due. When the call came, I was to go immediately on the bike. The old midwife neither biked nor drove a car, so she would have to follow on foot. It was a half-hour walk, maybe more in the snow. I was ready when the phone rang and made sure before I left that Sister was awake and aware that she was needed.

My hopes of a grateful reception when I reached the home

were soon squashed. I had made a point of not knocking the snow off my coat until someone had seen it, feeling that I was owed some sympathy for setting out in the middle of such an unpleasant night. Not that I had any choice, of course, and mum-to-be was not impressed, demanding to know, between contractions, if I was old enough to be delivering babies. It was not a good start and my patient was determined to do things her own way. Sister Morris and the baby arrived about the same time. She took the baby to care for while I attended to the mother. It all seemed to have gone well and I allowed myself a few seconds to think of the nice warm bed which I would be able to climb into in a couple of hours time. Then I noticed the blood.

The flying squad were efficient and kind. I sat on the edge of the bath, my white face in stark contrast to the crimson-stained water and blood soaked sheets floating gently in it. We knew these things could happen, but that didn't make it any easier to deal with. Previous deliveries had gone smoothly so this was a shock. A medic came in and perched at the side of me. "Don't worry, love," he said, "I've seen worse – not often, mind you, but she'll be alright."

With mother and baby on their way to hospital, Sister left for the long walk home, reminding me on her exit that it was today Women's Own were coming to interview us and take photos for a magazine article. I think it was to be called something like, The Benefits of a Home Delivery. That phrase seems to mean something quite different today, but of one thing I then was certain; the Flying Squad episode would not get a mention in the magazine. I cleared up wearily and put on my coat. Outside, it was almost light and the snow had stopped. Everything looked clean – like clean sheets and a fresh start.

A Remote Island in the Brasilian Rain Forest, 1978

The merciless sun beat down on a small boat as it chugged away from the riverbank. A hammock swayed to the boat's rhythm and perspiring relatives tried to steady it, touching its young occupant gently as though trying to instil some of their strength in her. Maria's skin was cold and clammy, her pale body past the stage where it would be warmed any more by the tropical heat. The boat tossed and pitched as it battled against the tide. Any whispers of conversation were drowned by the unseemly clattering of the engines, oblivious to the boat's sad cargo.

I stood on the shore with a few silent onlookers, watching. It was too late. I knew that. They should have gone hours ago when the bleeding first began.

Maria was married and just fifteen. Wizened old midwives, experience and tradition their only qualifications, had delivered the baby. Through the long, difficult labour, Maria had endured their rough handling, superstitious practices and ribald jokes. Relief set in as, eventually, the baby was born and could be passed round to be admired. It was relief which quickly turned to panic as the haemorrhage began. More unsavoury measures were embarked upon without success and, as often happened, I was called in as a last resort. The witchdoctors had long since exhausted their skills and mine were to prove ineffectual. The only hope for this young mother was the six-hour boat trip to the nearest medical post where there might be a doctor. After hours of delay and discussion, a boat was found and the small party set off with their tragic burden.

Even as we watched the boat getting smaller, we became aware of a break in its rhythmic movement. It was changing direction, straining against the waves. It slowly turned 180 degrees and began the short journey back to us.

Another fragile young life extinguished. Another motherless baby for already over burdened relatives to care for, but they would do it. They always did. Meanwhile, the ignorance and superstition would continue and more would die – unless something was done about it.

I decided I would try to put my training to good use. British nursing qualifications were not recognised in this part of the world, so anything I did would have to be unofficial, but basic midwifery classes, for anyone who would come, would start next week. Just maybe the next Maria would have a slightly better chance. There had been no flying squad for her, no hospital, just a waterlogged grave in a riverside cemetery. Her daughter should be twenty-seven now – if she has survived. I wonder if she thinks about the mother she never saw. I sometimes wonder if anyone still remembers her. I know I'll never forget.

Here and There – A Nurse Recollects

A mile-long road curves through the middle of Lowedges estate. Short roads and long crescents shoot off like the spine of a fish. Neat rows of houses, squat corner blocks of flats, maisonettes with balconied bedsits over them house the estate's population. A quarter of a mile in from each end of the main road is a small row of shops which, between them, cater for most basic daily requirements. Small clusters of residents chat to each other outside as they wait for the variety of buses that plough their way through at frequent intervals. One side the estate is served by the B6054, which heads out to Derbyshire; the other side, by a park and a golf course. Roughly in the middle of all this is the doctor's surgery.

The District Nursing Course is over. Six months supervised practice have been completed. I put on the navy blue dress, grab my Street Guide and diary and get into my battered red Fiesta for the first day's work.

Visit number one: Stitches

As I walk up the path to the house, I notice the neat garden, curtains held back with ties and a couple of ornaments on the sill. I look at the upstairs window and feel sure that must be my patient's bedroom. Boxes of games, figures of batman and the like are pressed against the pane. I can imagine the rest of the room. Daniel is eight years old. He fell off his bike a week ago, cutting his arm on a piece of glass. Today he is to have ten stitches removed. The white pvc door opens before my finger touches the bell.

"Hello, nurse." Mum looks anxious. "He's in there." I am gently pushed into the lounge. Daniel gives me an uncertain smile and his eyes have a touch of defiance in them. I set about carefully removing each tiny suture. Mum and I work as a team to keep up a stream of distracting conversation until the job is done. There are only a few "Ow's" and "Ouches" and the last stitch slides out. Now the smile is huge and I am invited to inspect the treasures in the bedroom. Minutes later I wave goodbye to my new friend, and, back in the car, check my diary to see who is next.

As I drive away my mind flashes back to another eight year old, Joshua. He lived on the tiny island of Bagre in one of the tributaries of the Amazon River in Brasil. As Joshua was carried into the front room of my small wooden house-on-stilts, the pungent smell of decay filled the place. His eyes were feverishly bright, his face anxious and his hand heavily bandaged with old rags. Parents and relatives soon filled the front room, closely followed by neighbours, who didn't want to miss out on anything interesting. They fixed the visitors black sweet coffee while I began to carefully remove the cloths. I felt sick with the smell and had huge butterflies in my stomach. A snake had bitten Joshua's hand, which was now a crumbling mass of damp, rotting flesh. Fingers were held on by threads. I cleaned it up as best I could, gave a penicillin shot and pleaded with the family to take him to the nearest town with a hospital, and hopefully, a doctor, though there was no guarantee of that. For poor people, it was a big undertaking. They agreed, though with apprehension. Doctors and hospitals were an unknown quantity to them, and to be treated with caution. We watched the small boat chug away on its seven – hour journey, and prayed there would be a doctor for them when they arrived.

Three months later, a bright little boy bounded up the steps into my house, followed by a smiling group of relatives. Joshua now had a stump instead of an arm, but he was very much alive.

Visit number two: Terminal Cancer

I find the next house without too much difficulty. The door is opened by a young woman. I follow her upstairs to a light, airy bedroom. The curtains, fluttering at the open window, match the bedding. The sheets are fresh. On the bed lies an older woman. Her husband sits by the bedside holding his wife's hand. He smiles, but pain shows in his eyes. I get the morphine ready and wait for my colleague to join me.

We chat quietly. The woman on the bed seems hardly aware of us, although we include her in the conversation. The door bell rings, followed by light footsteps on the stairs announcing the arrival of my colleague. Together we check the drug. The woman flinches as the sharp needle penetrates her thin arm. Soon she settles. She looks comfortable and cared for. We will be back in six hours time to give the next dose. We close the door quietly and chat for a few minutes before getting into our cars.

As I drive away, I remember Mary Edith.

Mary Edith lived on the Mocajuba River in the Amazon Rain Forest. There were no doctors or hospitals in this remote spot. Her thatch-roofed wooden house was stark and gloomy. One small window let in a few of the sun's rays. They bypassed the emaciated woman, who was lying in a dirty cotton hammock.

Her eyes were jaundiced, her voice just a whisper. She had been ill for some time, with only local healers and witch doctors to treat her. Low moans escaped from parched lips. The witch doctors crouched round the edge of the room, watching with hostility. On the floor stood a large tin bowl. The water in it was stained brown by the small pieces of twig and bark floating in it.

This, I was told, was to be given as an enema.

A gentle feel of the hugely distended abdomen confirmed my suspicion that a large, hard tumour had caused a complete blockage. Mary Edith was dying and not in a pleasant room with a clean bed and six-hourly injections of morphine. It was one drug not available over the counter in Brasil. The atmosphere was heavy with futility. I left all the codeine tablets I had with me, but knew it was just a gesture and probably wouldn't give her any more relief than the concoction in the bowl. I heard she died the following day.

Visit Number Three: Leg Ulcers

I climb the steps to the second floor flat and let myself in. My patient sits in a low armchair, both legs heavily wrapped with towels, which are now a soggy mess. We are down to our final hope of a cure for Maureen's leg ulcers. A new medication has just become available. I move the vase of daffodils from the small coffee table and set out my dressing packs. A clean striped towel is ready for me to wash my hands. We chat as I clean the wounds, put on the creams and then apply firm bandages, which will remain in place for three days. One leg is healing. The other is not. Maureen is a prisoner, unable to leave her home because of her grossly swollen, leaking legs. If this medication does not work, then an amputation will be offered as a final solution. She is not old. I feel sad as I leave, but at least we have things to try.

Old senor Saba's leg was wrapped in banana leaves. It didn't smell too good. Underneath, the ulcer was huge and deep. It had been there a long time. Getting it clean took awhile and Saba was not the most patient of men. Gradually, with various kinds of very basic remedies, the main ones being cleanliness and rest, the ulcer began to heal. Saba was not enjoying the daily dressing routine, and one day took off into the forest to hunt. When he came back a week later, the ulcer was much worse. The whole process began again, but every time we were almost there, a small scratch, a mosquito bite, and the whole thing flared up again.

One day Saba's dangerously old kerosene refrigerator caught fire. Quick action was needed to stop the whole wooden house going up in flames. As he manhandled the fridge to the open door and heaved it down the wooden steps onto the ground outside, Saba got badly burnt. The tiny island had no medical help. With local elections coming up, it was not too difficult to persuade the mayor to help. Votes count, even in far-flung places, and he had access to the only telephone in town.

A few hours later an old helicopter was gyrating drunkenly over the newly cut long grass, blowing it into the flimsy open houses and causing mini-tornadoes as the machine rocked gently to a standstill. Saba was quickly put on board along with some of the town's dignitaries, who were quick to seize the opportunity of a free trip to the Capital City, a four-hour flight away. This time the enforced rest did the trick. He returned three months later looking healthy, burns healed and with just a tiny scar where the ulcer had been.

After disappointing weeks of the new treatment with no progress made, Maureen decided to have the amputation and so passed out of my care. Three months later, I am delighted to bump into her in the street. She is smiling and off to the shops already managing her prosthesis like a pro.

Clinic – Lowedges

I look at my list. It tells me to expect several diabetics for blood sugar checks, small wounds that need dressing, blood pressures to take, people to weigh, three monthly vitamin injections to give, and a few minor ailments needing a little bit of treatment. The afternoon is not too demanding and the pay packet at the end of the month is very satisfactory.

Clinic – The Amazon

I didn't have a list so had no idea what to expect. People just came crowding into the front room from about seven am, completely disregarding the notice that said we didn't see folk before 8:30. They never came alone, always with a crowd of relatives.

Brasilian culture dictated that all visitors be served coffee, so a huge pot was made and constantly topped up during the day. Neighbours' children provided a washing up and waitress service, enjoying the free "entertainment" and their status as "family". The first patient, a child with malaria, was quickly followed by another with whooping cough, both killer diseases here. An elderly man with severe anaemia due to recurring malaria came next, followed by a young fisherman with a piranha bite, as big as an orange in circumference, on his chest. A tearful teenager entered, clutching his hand in which a barbed, poisonous fish spine was embedded.

The patients suffered stoically, grateful for the most basic help. Things were going smoothly until Benedito came in and minutes later I was to have my first experience of what was probably anaphylactic shock. Benedito had been bitten by a snake several days ago and the wound was not healing. I gave the usual penicillin injection and then watched in horror as he slumped to the floor. There was a gasp from the audience: " He's dead!"

It did look that way; he was certainly not breathing. The tray with the heart stimulant injection, which I always had ready but had never expected to use, was only a few feet away. The injection was quickly administered along with an antihistamine shot, which my teacher colleague injected at the same time. Our silent but frantic prayer for help flew heavenwards.

Benedito's chest moved, his eyes opened, and startled, he looked up at the fearful faces peering down at him. He was helped into a chair and given the obligatory cup of coffee, oblivious to the consternation he had caused. Soon he was on his way, surrounded by rather stunned relatives, with a few antihistamine pills in his pocket and dressings for his wound.

Meanwhile a sickly looking baby with dysentery was brought in and minutes later, an eight year old boy with a strange rash. The baby recovered, the little boy did not. My poor store of medicines were inadequate for meningitis. He died a week later on a tiny island at his witchdoctor grandmother's house, his family firmly refusing to seek medical help elsewhere.

Payment was voluntary at this clinic. At the end of the day we counted up our wages, all edible: two squawking chickens (both male); a turtle, alive; a piece of wild pig; four mangoes; a large plate of shrimp; a basket full of six inch long, wriggling, armour plated fish; a water melon and two alligator eggs. Not quite so neat as an NHS pay packet, but perhaps more precious when given by people who had very little for themselves. It would be a seafood supper tonight – when we had enlisted our neighbour's help to deal with the armour plated fish.

A Disastrous Weekend
Win Francis

"Can I go to Woodcraft Camp this weekend Mum?"

I was eleven years old and a new member of Firshill Woodcraft Folk group, recruited by my friend Irene.

"What will you need?" was Mum's response.

I was ready with a list of the necessary equipment and somehow we managed to scrape it all together. The camp was held most weekends during the summer months at Stubley Hollow on Bennett's farm at Dronfield Woodhouse.

We met at the Town Hall early on Saturday afternoon and went by tram to Meadowhead terminus. From there we walked through Greenhill village, down the path by the Transport Sports ground, and across the fields and Totley tunnel to the campsite. After dropping our rucksacks, we went up to the farm where the tents and other equipment were stored and, along with milk and water, we transported them down to the field.

"Gosh, these billies are heavy," I muttered to Irene.

"Here, we'll take those," said an older youth, and between them they made a chain and carried three billies between them. Would I ever be that tough, I wondered, and if so will my arms get longer with all that weight?

We then set to pitching the two-man tent that Irene and I were to share. It was one of about twenty, pitched in a semicircle along the edge of the field. With some adjustment of the guy ropes by the leader, he was satisfied that our tent would probably stay up overnight! So we put down our groundsheets and laid out our kit ready for evening inspection, known as "wappenshaw".

The first task of the afternoon was wooding, which was to collect enough wood for the weekend. It had to be dead wood, which is brittle and snaps easily, not green wood, which bends, does not burn well and creates a lot of smoke. We were given strict warnings against damaging trees, as they are living things and must be respected. Phew! There's a lot to learn about this camping lark! Wooding was only finished when the keeper of the woodpile was satisfied, and then we had free time until tea.

A small group had built a fire and suspended a billie of water between two wooden forks over the flames, and when it boiled, tea was brewed and we all sat in a circle for our evening meal. We had each taken enough food for the weekend (theoretically!) and the more experienced campers had brought tinned soup and tinned beans, which they heated on the embers of the fire. We envious "greensticks" had to make do with our sandwiches and cake. Oh well, we'll know better next time.

In the evening we built a large pagoda campfire at the bottom corner of the field. This was in a small hollow surrounded by little hillocks, and after the fire lighting ceremony, we sat on these mounds to sing songs and do skits. The highlight for me was a ghost story told by Brown Eagle, the group leader and camp headman. He had a wonderful way of telling a yarn, which made the hair stand up at the back of our impressionable necks.

After a final song and "leave-take" it was time for bed, and with much giggling Irene and I made the most of our blankets with safety pins and crawled inside.

Shortly after came "silence cry", which sounded very eerie in the quiet of the night, and the camp settled down to sleep. I could feel every bump and stone in the ground beneath. The blanket was thin and the night air cold and soon I was shivering and feeling very lonely.

"Are you awake?" I whispered to Irene. There was no reply, only the steady breathing of a peaceful sleeper. I tried to snuggle up to her for warmth, but it had little effect. I could see branches through the tent silhouetted against the moonlit sky, only adding to my feeling of desolation. Suddenly, an owl screeched and I was back in the ghost story, completely terrified. I tried to reason with myself that there were children younger than I in the nearby tents, and I didn't hear any of them whimpering with fear.

I eventually started to drift off into a fitful sleep when I was jolted back to wakefulness by slow footsteps and heavy breathing outside. There was a sudden "twang" on the guy rope and a dark shape loomed over the tent followed by a rasping and snuffling noise. I imagined some fearful dragon-like creature trying to get in the tent to carry me off to its lair. I frantically shook Irene who sat bolt upright and said, "What's the matter?"

"There's something outside trying to get in," I trembled, clutching hold of her. At that moment there was a cough and soft moo.

"It's only a cow, you idiot. They wander in from the next field. It'll go if we ignore it."

"I'm frozen," I said. "I can't sleep."

"Right. Put on all the clothes that you've got with you and we'll snuggle in together." And with that, we combined our blankets and rolled up in them like a couple of Egyptian mummies.

We must have fallen asleep because the next thing we heard was "morning cry" and we were up and off for a cold wash at the stream with all the other campers.

The Woodcraft Folk have ceremonies based on ancient folklore, which appealed to my romantic soul. After breakfast we laid our kit out neatly for morning wappenshaw, which was followed by morning council. This was a meeting of all campers from the youngest to the oldest and everyone had the right to be heard if they wished. The various camp officers gave their reports, from the state of the latrines to the general tidiness of the site, and then the day's programme was decided.

We were given a choice of various activities with the aim of improving our "woodcraft". For example: plant and flower recognition, tree identification, tracking using country signs, each of which could lead to a badge when a certain standard was reached. This was followed by active games like volleyball, gymnastics, races and general letting off steam.

It was during this period that I was being chased by one of the boys in a game of tiggy, and in my determination not to be caught, I ran towards a patch of scrub which dropped away at the bottom of the field. Too late, I heard the cry of warning as I ran full tilt up to my knees in a bog. I was horrified and struggled wildly to free myself, only seeming to get deeper in the mire. Someone shouted to me to stand still, and two of the bigger lads shook off their slippers and waded in to grab my hand to pull me out. The three of us floundered about, me in a panic, they struggling to free me, and all the others shouting advice from the sidelines.

With a great deal of squelching and sucking noises we all eventually extricated ourselves from the mud, covered in the stuff. The only problem was, I was minus one shoe! My first thought was "What will Mum say? I haven't had them long," and I burst into anguished tears. Several of the older youths, seeing my distress, decided to go in and search for my missing shoe, but it was a forlorn hope and despite poking around with sticks, and digging with their feet, my shoe was determined to stay buried in the bog. We all had to wash in the stream to get rid of the smelly muck, and by this time some of my enthusiasm for camping was beginning to wane. I had to borrow a pair of plimsolls to walk home in and was dreading explaining to Mum how I had lost one of my shoes. I knew that they were an expensive item to buy from Dad's meagre wages at the foundry.

Time may have mellowed my memory of the reception I received, but Mum was always a kind soul, and I think that seeing my mortification, she thought I had suffered enough. Needless to say, though, that was the last Woodcraft camp I went to for some years – in fact, till I rejoined at the age of sixteen. I then spent the next fifty or so years off and on in the "Folk," met my husband, raised my family and had some of the happiest times of my life.

Nowhere To Go
Minnie Douglas

It was a cold night. My bedroom was very dark. The candle had gone out. I daren't get out of bed to open the curtains, but hunched under the covers, my teeth chattering.

Once again my mother and step-father were fighting.

My mother was only trying to protect herself. My step-father had been drinking again.

I was so frightened he would kill her. When I was grown up, I would leave and never come back. I could smell the fumes of the beer. The odour seemed to pervade the whole house.

Suddenly, I sprang out of bed and started to descend the stairs. No one could hear me with all the noise coming from their bedroom. As I reached the bottom stair there was a sudden screech as I trod on the cat. I stood still. My heart was thudding fit to burst. Now I was hot, sweating with fear, feeling around the room for my shoes. I could not light the gas mantle so just fumbled around in the dark for my coat.

Once again I trod on the poor cat. No wonder they have nine lives. My brother had saved this one from drowning. It had been thrown into a stream, tied in a bag with its brothers and sisters. He was the only one alive. But this was before my mother had married and brought this brute of a man into our home. I had step-brothers and sisters, who, because of lack of space, stayed in their former home. They knew what their father was like and did not see him much.

I had an older sister who had just got married and that was where I was going. I found the door, reached for the lock, turned the key and opened the door, not bothering to close it. I ran as fast as I could to my sister's home and told her what was happening. She kissed and cuddled me and put me to bed. I learned next day that she and her husband had visited my home and sorted my step-father out.

Peace did not last long. My step-father warned me that if I did this again, it would be me on the end of his fist. My mother still had black eyes and bruises and would groan if you touched her. I was always worried about her, but she always stayed with him. She had nowhere else to go.

Aunt Ada's Visit
Bet Bullock

One of my strongest childhood memories is the day my Aunt Ada paid us a visit. Although her name came up occasionally during family conversations, no one had seen her for many years. She wasn't really my aunt, she was my father's eldest brother's daughter, which made her my cousin, but Uncle George married and had children in his twenties, whereas my father was forty four when I was born. Thus, the day I met her, I was eleven, my sister Joan fourteen, whilst Ada, according to my mother, wouldn't see thirty again.

Both my sister and I were anxious to meet her, as her past was shrouded in mystery. The only information we were able to glean was that she had married and divorced within two years and left home under a cloud. She was man-mad, said my mother, but my father, for some reason, had a soft spot for her and refused to hear a bad word said.

We had just finished having tea when we heard the tooting of a horn and, looking through the front window, saw a car had pulled up at our gate. And what a car! It was big, white and had two shiny chrome head lamps. 'Good Lord,' said Dad, 'it's a Bentley!" As he spoke, a tall man wearing a camel coat and a fedora got out and walked round to the passenger side. I couldn't see much of his face because of the brim of his hat, but I did see he had a thin moustache, and thought he looked just like Ronald Coleman, and said so. My sister cuffed me and told me not to be ridiculous. Then a woman stepped out of the car. I gasped. She was wearing a cloche type hat and a long black coat with a big white fur collar. (My sister told me later it was silver fox). I was convinced that they were film stars. They both came through the gate and down the path.

My dad rushed to the front door saying, 'Good God, it's Ada!'

I moved to go after him but my mum pulled me back. 'You two

go and sit on the couch and behave yourselves,' she said, and with that she followed Dad. Very reluctantly, my sister and I sat on the horsehair sofa, not only because we were eager to see our visitors, but also the sofa was uncomfortable and scratchy. (On the very next Guy Fawkes night I set it on fire with some sparklers, but that's another story.) From being excited, I suddenly got nervous, as I was shy with strangers. This usually manifested itself by my being struck dumb initially, and then over-compensating by behaving in a childishly frenetic manner.

My sister, knowing me well, hissed in my ear, 'If you show us up, I'll kill you. Just say hello and then keep quiet.'

There was the sound of laughter from the hall and a husky voice said, 'Oh, Jack! You haven't changed, have you? How do you put up with him Grace?'

The living room door opened as my mum said, 'I've got used to it after twenty odd years. Anyway, come and meet the children.' She was first in the room and I noticed she wasn't smiling. My dad was though, grinning from ear to ear, as he ushered the couple in.

My sister and I stood up. 'Joan, Betty, meet your Aunty Ada and her friend Ray,' said my dad. My aunt rushed forward, hugged and kissed my sister and then did the same to me. I was conscious in that moment of soft lips, wonderful perfumey smells and the soft silky fur of her collar tickling my nose. On being released I heard my sister say hello, but, despite her dire warnings, I just stood there gaping like an idiot.

My aunt chuckled, 'Cat got your tongue?' and then everybody laughed. I don't remember much of what was said after that. I think I was spoken to and probably answered, but I was totally in awe of this beautiful woman from another world. I kept saying to myself, 'She's my aunty, my aunty!' I watched her long fingers with painted nails take out a cigarette from a slim flat box and place it between her red lips. Ray leaned forward with a gold lighter, and when it was lit she removed it from her mouth, tilted her head upward, pouted her lips and blew out a steady stream of fine blue smoke. For days afterwards I found myself mimicking her actions using a pencil.

I don't how long this fantastic pair stayed with us but I was suddenly aware that everybody was on their feet moving about and saying their goodbyes. My sister and I were kissed again and my dad escorted Ada and Ray to their car. We watched them through the window; my dad shook hands with Ray and hugged my aunt. We waved as they drove off.

When my dad came back in my mother said something to him in a low voice and they both disappeared into the kitchen. Voices were raised and a door slammed. I looked at my sister for answers, but she shrugged and went upstairs. Left alone, I was mystified and couldn't understand the sudden change from the warmth I'd felt and the laughter I'd heard. I couldn't decide whether to go into the kitchen to my mum or upstairs to my sister; I chose the latter.

My sister was sat in front of the dressing room mirror combing her hair. (I don't like saying it but my sister was rather vain). I sat on the bed and asked her to tell me what was wrong. At first she refused, but finally told me that it was obvious. My mum was upset because Ada had never stopped preening and posing and telling us what a wonderful life she had in Blackpool with Ray. My dad had behaved like a silly schoolboy, hanging on her every word, and my mother and Joan had been totally ignored. Ray was a dance band leader, he'd played in the Tower several times, but despite their fancy clothes and accents they were, in her opinion, both as cheap as muck. (I felt like arguing about that but didn't want to put her off telling me the rest). Our mum, when she could get a word in, had asked Ada if she had visited her mum and dad but was told not likely, because as far as she was concerned they no longer existed after the way they treated her following her divorce. She (Ada that is) realised now, having met intelligent people, that her parents were ignorant and living in the Middle Ages. The only person in the family who'd showed her any kindness had been our dad, who had been sensible enough to get away from it all, join the army and learn a thing or two. He was the reason she was here. She and Ray were staying at the Grand Hotel tonight and going back to Blackpool tomorrow.

Mum only spoke once more, when she asked if Ada and Ray were going to get married. They both laughed. Ada said Ray was married already but separated, and they were living together. Our mum looked shocked, which seemed to amuse Ada, and Dad didn't come to Mum's rescue. 'As for you,' my sister went on, 'it was as if you were hypnotised! I told you to close your mouth twice but you obviously didn't hear me. The whole thing's been a disaster and I wish she'd never come here.' She finished by saying, 'Now go away and read your film magazines and for goodness sake, grow up!'

I left feeling totally bewildered and went and sat in my favourite hiding place, on the landing window ledge behind long curtains. I was sad that my mum and dad were cross with each other but I still felt bewitched by my aunty. She can't be all that bad, I thought, not looking like she does, and it crossed my mind that my sister was peeved because she didn't get a look in. I decided to stay put until my sister went downstairs and then write it all down in my diary.

My aunty never visited us again. We went on holiday to Blackpool the following year but both Ada and Ray had left there by then. I did see her once again though. It was nine years later and I was on leave from the WAAF. My father had died in the August just before war broke out in September '39, and my mother had remarried. I hated my step-father, and, although she didn't say so, I think my mum knew she'd made a mistake. Fortunately, he was at work during the day, so we went out a lot together and on one occasion I mentioned Aunty Ada's visit.

Mum didn't want to talk about it, as it had caused the first real quarrel between her and my dad they'd ever had. I asked her if she'd always disliked Ada, and she said no, but she'd envied her, and was a bit jealous of her relationship with my dad. Mum told me that the last she'd heard of Ada was that she had returned to Sheffield and was living in a bungalow with two brothers. The story was that both brothers were in love with her, and she in turn loved them both. She'd tried to patch things up with her parents but they still refused to own her, even after she had married one of the brothers. I found out her address from one of my cousins and decided to visit her.

I called on my aunt and stayed about an hour. Both the brothers were at work. My aunt no longer looked like a film star. She wore no make-up and her hair was no longer in neat Marcel waves. She still talked and laughed a lot but now she was just plump and jolly. I asked her, was it true that her parents had disowned her just because she left her husband? She said yes, her mother had said you've made your bed, you must lie on it. Oh, I lay on it all right, she told me, every night when he came home drunk he laid me out on it. I've still got the scars to prove it, and they knew what he was like, they knew.

I also asked her how she decided which brother to marry if she loved them both, or why she'd bothered to get married at all. She said it was the brothers' idea; they'd talked it over and decided there was too much gossip and snide remarks about her down at the local pub. They would still share her though, but be discreet, so it would give her a certain amount of respectability. Not that she cared in the slightest, but it stopped them coming home with bruises and black eyes. I saw shades of my old aunty when she gave a low chuckle and said she'd refused to choose which one to marry so they'd tossed a coin, best out of three. We both laughed and she gave me a big hug when I left.

This time though there were no soft lips, wonderful perfumery smells or silky fur. I went away no longer star-struck, for I'd grown up, learnt a thing or two and knocked about a bit myself. I think I knew then what attracted my father to her. She was a warm and loving woman, but also a woman before her time, a woman who felt at ease in her own skin. A free spirit.

Second Parting
Bet Bullock

The old man nipped out his cigarette, placed the stub in a small tin box, hitched up the flap of his overcoat and slid the box into his trouser pocket. He looked around; no one was in sight.

Taking a newspaper from his topcoat pocket, he carefully bent forward and placed it, half-folded, on the ground, and, more carefully still, sank to his knees, landing squarely in the centre of the paper. He picked up a vase, half-filled with water, which stood to one side and placed it on a stone slab at the base of a white headstone. His gnarled hand shook a little as, from the other side, he grasped a bunch of chrysanthemums, causing a few petals to fall on the grass. He dropped the flowers into the vase, moving them from side to side with one finger until they were evenly spread. Satisfied with the result, he bowed his head.

'Bessie love, here I am again old girl, here again as usual.' He hesitated, cleared his throat and went on. 'It's a bit different this time though, not just a chat, sommat I've got to tell you and I wish I 'adn't. Now don't start worrying before I say owt, you allus were a whittler. Are you ready? Well….here goes then.

'It's nigh on two years since you die - since you were tecken from me, that is. Anyway, Bessie love, things aren't too good. Look, I know I've been tellin' you I'm all right and I 'ave been, honest - well, as good as can be expected at my age I suppose. Anyway, lately, I've been a bit shaky on mi pins, unsteady like. Now then, our lass, I know what you're thinkin'. To many visits t'Crown an' Anchor. Well, you're wrong. I still only go twice a week for a couple of pints and a game of dommies as afore. Any'ow, what it boils down to is, I tripped and fell, cut my head on t'cooker. It weren't but a scratch. I've 'ad a sight worse many a time. But it set 'em thinking I shun't live on mi own. It were that lass from social that finally put kybosh on it, told Jimmy all about it, rang all way to London she did and next thing I knew, 'im and that la-di-da wife of 'is were knockin' on front door.'

The old man felt a twinge of pain in his left knee, so paused to shift his weight.

'Where were I...oh aye, well, I'll not drag it out love, upshot is our Jimmy, James as she calls 'im, has put our 'ouse up for sale and got me fixed up in an 'owd folk's home down south near their place. They don't know this, but I was in t'kitchen and heard our Jimmy say 'e still didn't know why I couldn't live with them and she told 'im not to be so stupid – what would their friends think? Huh! I wouldn't 'ave lived with 'er at any price, I'd put missen in workhouse first.

'Look. I don't want you to blame our Jimmy, 'e's a good lad, allus 'as bin, but 'is life's not 'is own now. Any road up, they tell me this home is a good 'un, I'll 'ave me own room and telly and all me meals got ready so I'll be well tecken care of. She said me smokes might 'ave to go but we'll see about that. Anyway, Jimmy's promised me, on quiet like, flower's'll come reglar and grass'll be cut anall so everything'll be nice and tidy 'ere for you duck.'

He reached for his handkerchief and blew his nose noisily. 'I'm gonna miss coming 'ere, but well, we've 'ad a good run old girl, 'aven't we, and anyhow I don't reckon it'll be long afore I join you proper like, so, it's tara for now love and God bless.'

The old man continued to kneel for a moment, then, pressing the ground with both hands, slowly and painfully balanced first on one leg and then the other, and pulled himself erect. His face was pale and drawn, his eyes glistened and a teardrop rolled down his cheek and dropped unnoticed on to the lapel of his greatcoat. One last look: Elizabeth Harper, Beloved Wife of Joseph William Harper. He read no more, having read it a hundred times. He bent to pick up the newspaper, wincing as his knees and back protested, then, turning slowly, he threaded his way through a row of gravestones to the path beyond.

In the Garden
Jean Allen

I sit on the step, French doors open behind me, voile curtains fluttering in the breeze.
A fountain splashes noisily.
A small wrought iron table and two chairs wait for visitors.
Pots filled with geraniums stand about haphazardly on weathered flagstones.
Tiny weeds wriggle up between cracks.
Roses and clematis wrestle gently with each other along the walls.
Small stone statues peep out from behind the shrubs,
An exotic bay tree rustles its leaves above me.
The tropical palm scratches my arm.
Mediterranean yukka and cordyline stand sentry-like on the steps.
Japanese maples shimmer in the hazy heat.
Below my feet, a pebbled water feature bubbles and froths.
The breeze catches hold of a handful of water and throws it mischievously onto the skinny ginger tom taking his nap in the sun. He leaps up indignantly and stalks off to find more secure shelter under a large fern.
The scent of rosemary, lavender and thyme drift past.
Butterflies flutter.
Birds swoop.
Dragonflies hover.
I sip cool lemon tea from a blue china cup and close my eyes.
I could be anywhere.
I'm in my garden on Lowedges, of course.

Worlds Apart
Jean Allen

Her role and mine, how different!
Thousands of miles apart, on separate continents,
our expectations divide us as effectively as the ocean.
She is the village teacher,
her school a flimsy, wooden room on stilts.
Rain forest presses in on three sides, the river on the fourth – the
  only road.
Her students travel by canoe
this simple school their hope of brighter futures.
From them she has respect. Too soon the midday sun
drives all to seek the shade.
Thick, black coffee is her only lunch
and then she follows him down forest trail
to tend their small plantation, gathering their meagre evening
  meal.
Dusk falls and, homeward bound,
he strides ahead, knife flashing in the suns last rays.
She follows him, the fair haired, fair skinned teacher
stooping as she walks.
She is ten years his senior and her basket is heavy.
"I rule," he seems to say, "she serves."
And for some recognition of her worth
she waits, encouraged by their eagerness
'til morning brings her students up the river.

I sit at my computer screen,
around me, comforts; I have choices, friends.
and if I choose to marry, it will be not as a trophy, prized but
  never loved.
We seem to live in different centuries –
no prospects, no ambition hers except the humble school,

while I fly high, assert my rights, express opinions and enjoy
 respect.
I often wonder how my life, and hers, would be
If she had been born here, and I had been born there?
Would she have been headmistress
valued for her skills, esteemed by many?
And what of me – would I have been like her,
unable to escape the forest's clutches, life dull with drudgery
 and toil?
Or could I have embarked in my canoe
and let the river carry me to Samba Schools and beaches,
carnivals – a million miles away from both our worlds?

The Pin
Irene Ward

Don't you think that life is like looking for a pin?
You search around and search around to see which drawer it's in.
I'll bet you never find it, no matter how you try.
That pin is safely tucked away from your exploring eye.
But one day when you're unaware, that sly elusive pin
will look at you as if to say, "This is the drawer I'm in."

The Master Craftsman
Jean Allen

"Building bridges is a God- like thing to do
Joining islands, making one instead of two.
God, if he came here,
Would be an engineer.
He came
and was."

His hands were calloused, as he plied his trade
A chair, a table, baby's cot he made.
Broken hearts he could repair
save people from despair,
still does,
loves us.

Hewing crosses is a man – like thing to do.
I wonder Roman gibbet who made you?
Would I, if I'd been there
have taken time to care?
and think,
"Why this?"

Great craftsman, maker of the universe,
my cosmic God, who mourns creation's curse.
You built a bridge, your plan,
A path from God to man.
A cross.
Your loss.
My gain.

I heard the 1st verse quoted at a conference and have not been able to find out who wrote it. Many thanks to her or him, in any case!

Love
Win Francis

Your love is a comfy dressing gown that wraps me in its warm embrace.
It is a well thumbed book I never tire of reading.
It is a rainbow arching across the wide blue sky,
and the comfort of an easy chair that rests my weary bones.
Your love is the bus that comes when I am tired of waiting at the stop.
It is the hand that takes the heavy shopping bag from me.
It is the gentle breeze that cools
me when I am hot and bothered,
and the fire that warms me when I come in from the cold.

My love is a woollen scarf that comforts you on winter days.
It's the cool refreshing drink when you come in from the garden.
It's the hand that massages your aching shoulders
and the answer to your crossword clue.
It is the comfy pillow where you rest your weary head
and the pile of freshly ironed shirts waiting to be put away.
My love is sharing the newspaper on Sunday morning
and the companionable silence.
It is a comfy pair of shoes, well worn but well polished.

Our love is Stannage Edge, as firm and enduring as the stone that stands there.

Flight
Win Francis

I sometimes dream that I can fly and leave the mundane earth behind,
I simply raise my arms aloft and I am floating on the wind.
My arms are wings and I can soar or dive however the fancy takes me.
This is my world and I am one with heaven's enormous canopy.
With effortless ease, I'm over the trees, the arching sky above me
and in the vast expanse of blue, powder puff clouds are my company.
No bird flies with me, I travel alone, sole passenger in the heavens
solitude and silence treasured in my peaceful haven.
The air is soft upon my face and fragrant with the summer's scent
I revel in my new-found skill, exploring God's wide firmament.
I leave my worries far below, this is so far from earthly woe.
If I should die whilst dreaming thus
t'would be a lovely way to go.

Just an Ordinary Family

Becky Bollet, Republican

(no names, no pack drill)

'Damnation!' exclaims Flip. 'The eggs are runny again.'

Ellie stabs at a piece of bacon, which flies off her plate. Flip sticks out his left hand and catches it.

'Howzat!' He pops the recalcitrant morsel into his mouth.

'Oh dear,' says Ellie sadly. 'One does get tired of remonstrating with one's kitchen staff. This is the fourth chef we've had this year.'

'The trouble is,' replies Flip, spearing a sausage and sawing through its burnt exterior, 'all they teach them today is that cordon bleu muck we have to suffer when we entertain. Thank God there's an excellent cafe not far away that provides a perfect breakfast.'

Ellie lays down her knife and fork and dabs her lips with a serviette. 'And how do you know that?'

'Ah!' says Flip, munching away, 'how careless of me! Now it's confession time. In your absence I've had the odd take away.'

'But you never have any money.'

'Unnecessary, it's on the house.'

'Oh no!' cries Ellie. 'Think of the publicity.'

'Not to worry, old girl, we have an agreement.'

'What kind of agreement?'

'The proprietor's father-in-law has a large allotment and is getting weary of following the Life Guards with a bucket and shovel scraping up their droppings. I have arranged for him to collect as much horse shit and straw as he wishes from our stables.'

'Mm,' muses Ellie, 'it would still make a good story for the press. I can see the headline now: Shit for Breakfast at the Palace.'

Flip shrugs. 'I'd deny it and threaten litigation.'

'But we'll never sue.'

'Never say never. Fifty years ago, divorce in the family was taboo.'

They eat in silence - well, comparative silence, there being the odd burp and clicking of teeth.

'Well, I hope you're right. We are constantly in the newspapers as it is. What with young Ginger cheating at marbles and Pandy being seen with numerous women hanging on his arm.

Flip picks up a slice of bread and mops up the remains on his plate. 'The marbles affair is a damn lie,' he says firmly.

'But what about the video?' Ellie says anxiously. 'It clearly shows Ginger pointing to the sky and his tutor rearranging the marbles while everybody is gazing upward.'

Flip bangs his fist on the table, causing all the Tupperware to wobble alarmingly. 'It's a bloody fake!' he shouts. 'Just like those of Chuck and his bird.'

Ellie's lower lip trembles. 'Oh, I do wish mummy were here. I miss her advice.' Flip piles marmalade on to a slice of toast.

'I'm sure you do my dear. Her mind was as sharp as a tack…..most of the time. By the way, I think Teddy's up to his old tricks. I saw him sneaking around in the garden with his video camera.'

'Are you sure it was him?'

'Quite sure. He'd attempted some sort of disguise but I'd recognise that bald dome of his anywhere.'

'Did you accost him?'

'No way. I instructed the gardener to set the dogs on him.'

Flip picks up a knife. He scrapes up the marmalade which has fallen from his toast and puts it back into the jar.

Ellie picks up the teapot. 'Would you like me to be mother?'

'Mine or yours?' cracks Flip.

'Flip by name and flippant by nature. Do be sensible, hubby dear, your jokes are in bad taste and becoming more frequent in your dotage.'

She pours out two cups of tea.

'Huh!' says Flip peevishly, 'I'm the least of your worries.

What about that red-haired virago, flaunting herself as usual. Charity my arse! When did she ever do anything for nothing?'

'Thank goodness Billy is a good boy,' says Ellie smiling. 'At least we have no worries there.'

'Not yet,' says Flip gloomily. 'Where did we go wrong?'

'Perhaps you and I being related was a mistake. They do say it can cause problems,' proffers Ellie.

She dips a Rich Tea biscuit into her tea.

'Fiddlesticks!' roars Flip.

Bits of marmalade and bread fly from his mouth.

'Do use your serviette before you speak,' says Ellie tartly, 'and where are the ginger biscuits I ordered? The staff know they're my favourites.'

'You're far too lax with them. They take advantage of your good nature to do as they please. I'll get our daughter to have a word with them, she'll shake them up.'

'She hardly ever pops in to see us since she remarried.'

'Put a stop on her allowance, she'll call quick enough.' He leans back and relaxes. 'Anyway, what's on the worksheet today?'

'You're going to Plymouth. Another one of your reunions. It seems no time at all since you had one in Portsmouth.'

'Got to keep in touch with the old crew. Not many of us left. What are you doing?'

'I'm opening that very expensive building in Scotland, something to do with politics, must bone up on it on the plane. Suppose I'd better get the old tartan out of mothballs. Hey ho, a woman's work is never done. I don't suppose you'd like to swap places?'

Flip roars with laughter. 'Not on your nelly. I used to think otherwise, but not being the boss has definite advantages.'

Any similarity to any person or persons, alive or dead is not coincidental but names have been changed to protect the guilty.

(With apologies to the Royles)

A Letter from Hospital to her Writer's Workshop Classmates

Irene Pryor

Hello, girls. Thank you for the lovely, lovely card and the sentiments expressed. Bless you all, I had a few happy tears. However, I'm really doing well now and I hope it won't be too long before I see my darling Minnie and my beloved Pat, plus all the rest of the Golden Girls.

I have been ill; quite hairy, in fact, it was. Actually, if you remember, I've been whingeing about not feeling well since Christmas. My blood count had dropped like a stone, and my blood pressure was doing a Jack the Giant Killer climbing up the beanstalk. So I had three blood transfusions. At one time, I felt so bad I thought I was going to die, until I realised how unpleasant that was, so I decided to make a better effort. It worked, and I have survived.

David, my son, has been pure twenty-four carat gold. I would not change him for his weight in diamonds. He took charge of everything, he was there when I fell. My daughter Georgina flew straight away from Ireland. She told me afterwards that, though David was coping with everything, he was terrified because he thought he might lose me. Georgina says, "Mother, you must try not to be so willful and independent! You worry David so much. I thank God for my brother every night of my life and I'm not having you worrying and upsetting him."

Pretty strong talk, but I can see her point and I think it's time I accepted help, especially now.

I have decided to have a coat of arms – two crossed hypodermic needles over a zimmer frame rampart.

I will write again and we shall meet again I know.

Much love from Fanlight Fanny, the frowsy bedpan queen.

No Flies on our Bread Cakes Last Term
Irene Pryor

It was nineteen-twenty-seven and I was twelve years old. My parents moved house. I had to leave the school I had attended and join another one nearer to our new house.

The new school was completely different to the previous one. It was co-educational, meaning both boys and girls in the same classes, a headmaster and mostly male teachers. I had, during juniors, been at a girl's school, so things were uncomfortable for me to say the least. Also, the attitude of the pupils towards education was something I had never experienced before.

The district where we came to live was lower working class. (Though we had not really been up market before, it was suburban and better class.) It was strange and not what I was used to at all. My fellow pupils had a far different idea of street wisdom than I had. Actually, I doubt I was street wise at all.

On the first day of the new term – I had just joined the school – Mr. Linton, the headmaster, brought Mr. Lederer into our classroom.

"A new member of staff," he said, "to teach you singing." The class was doubtful; still, we all chanted, "Good morning Mr. Lederer" after he had bidden us the same, saying,"Good morning Class Five." We left it at that. We were not impressed. On the following Friday afternoon, when we walked into class after playtime, Mr. Lederer was at his desk, prepared to teach us singing. His method was to stand against the desk and wave his baton, working up a fine perspiration. This was not all. We nearly jumped out of our seats when he bashed the baton down on the desk just as we were in mid-note.

"Shakespeare must be revolving in his grave," he said. We were supposed to be singing *Where the bee sucks there suck I*, while Miss Sharpe accompanied us on the piano.

Miss Sharpe, who had stopped playing the piano, probably as

shocked as we were, began again. We did a couple of lines, then **crash**! The desk was bashed again.

"We have one here who is tone deaf," said Mr. Lederer. There was, we knew, but we were not going to split. It was Jack Parkinson – not only tone deaf, but he sang like an amorous bull frog. It was not long before Mr. Lederer found Jack and his non-melodious voice. Jack was removed to outside the classroom door, where he spent the rest of the lesson breathing on the glass and writing rude words with his finger. This left marks and the caretaker complained.

Mr. Linton said, "Just one small incident in the battle to get some education into their heads," meaning our heads of course. The caretaker disagreed, and high words followed. The caretaker did not give notice but it was a near thing.

We were delighted. Of course, Jack got the cane. He showed us the marks. We were speechless with admiration. One bold soul ventured to ask, "Wottle yer dad seh?"

"Wot mi dad dun't no won't urt 'im," Jack said. "Our Colin nose if 'e splits ah'l bash 'is 'ed in. T'others' ull seh nowt. Any ow, mi dad ud on'y tek 'is belt off ter mi fer trunatin. Ah'd ony get a clout from't cane."

It was the first time I knew about caning. At the girl's school, I don't think they had one. Not that we were angels. Punishment meant we had to learn long passages from Shakespeare. Primarily, we were supposed to work hard, pass the Eleven Plus, go on to Grammar School and hopefully, to University. Of course, not everyone passed, but a good percentage did so. At the co-educational school, if anyone passed, very few went on to higher education. Their parents just could not afford to send them.

We did not object to the strict discipline or the cane, but it was the desk bashing and the sarcasm. So Mr. Lederer was going to be sent up. In my ignorance, at first I didn't know what was going on, but on the principle of, "If you can't beat 'em, join 'em", I finally caught on.

If it had been written work, we would never have got away with it. Parents and teaching staff had to be coped with. Parents dismissed art, drama and music as *mucking about*, a waste of time; history and geography were not much use to a girl working in a factory, or a boy going into the steel works or down a mine. Reading, writing and reckoning were what we were at school for, and as soon as we had mastered these, better to leave school at thirteen and get out and earn our living.

The Friday afternoon following the one when Jack got the cane, Mr. Lederer began again. This time it was *Greensleeves*. He bashed the desk.

"If Henry the eighth heard you, you would all be in the tower awaiting execution," he said. We had scored. We were not stupid. We knew how to sing flat. On with, *Drink to me only with thine eyes*. Miss Sharpe's idea of playing the piano was to rest all her considerable weight on the loud pedal. We yelled through the song at the tops of our voices to drown her out. Mr. Linton complained.

"Something must be done about this noise," he said. "The rest of the school cannot do their lessons. They can't hear their teachers."

The weeks went on. *By cool Siloam's shady glen* – bash! went the baton. It was the descant this time.

"You sound like a lot of fighting cats," said Mr. Lederer. That was exactly what we intended it to sound like. *Now is the month of Maying, when merry lads are playing* wasn't too bad until we came to the twiddly bits. Bash! went the baton on the desk. Mr. Lederer's blood pressure rose by leaps and bounds. He beat a tattoo on the desk. It sounded superb. It was during *Ye banks and braes of bonnie Doon* that the desk gave up the struggle. Splinters began to fly off. Those in the front desks took to holding their songbooks two inches from their noses. We were promised *The Floral Dance* but it never came to anything. School closed for the Christmas holidays.

It was barely a week after we had gone back to school. We knew Mr. Lederer had left. Rumour had it that he suffered a nervous breakdown. Most of us thought that was pushing it. Still, you never know, and as Jack Parkinson said, "There weren't no flies on our bread cakes last term." We agreed, and quietly filed in to assembly to sing our morning hymn.

Friendship
Barbara Thackeray

My friend has a heart of gold.
She's the dearest treasure this world could hold,
there for me when I feel down.
For sympathy she takes the crown
and for the times I've cause to worry
she's always there to say, "I'm sorry."
And when there are times to celebrate
of course she's there
'Cos she's my mate.